ALTAR GUILD
HANDBOOK

ALTAR GUILD HANDBOOK

S. Anita Stauffer

Fortress Press   **Philadelphia**

Library of Congress Cataloging in Publication Data

Stauffer, S. Anita.
  Altar guild handbook.

  Includes index.
  1. Altar guilds—Handbooks, manuals, etc.
I. Title.
BV195.S69 1985 247 85-47713
ISBN 0-8006-1868-8

Printed in the United States of America   1-1868

94   93   6   7   8   9   10

Te Deum Laudamus

Contents

1

A Place for Worship

You are God; we praise you.
You are the Lord; we acclaim you.
You are the eternal Father; all creation worships you.

—Te Deum, Lutheran Book of Worship

For nearly two thousand years, God's baptized people have gathered each Sunday morning to worship—to acknowledge that God is the Holy One, and to praise and acclaim him: "You are God; we praise you." We gather to worship in order to adore our Creator and Redeemer. We worship God simply because he is God, because he is worthy of being praised.

Worship is our adoring response to the Holy One whom we call God. Worship is our encounter with this God—and with each other in God's presence. Worship is the central and unique function of the church; without worship, there would be no church. Worship identifies the church *as* the church.

To worship, the baptized community assembles with awe in the presence of the Almighty. To worship is to remember the incarnation of our Lord and to sing with the angels, "Glory to God in the highest!" It is to recall the crucifixion and resurrection and to sing, "Worthy is Christ, the Lamb who was slain." It is to stand in the awesome presence of God and to sing,

"Holy, holy, holy Lord, God of power and might: heaven and earth are full of your glory." It is to be renewed and nourished with Christ's body and blood and to sing with thanksgiving, "Lord, now you let your servant go in peace; your word has been fulfilled."

In corporate worship we celebrate the saving acts of God—in creation, in history, and in our own lives. We gather to remember and give thanks for all that God has done for his people through the ages. We assemble in God's presence, we acknowledge God's holiness, we remember God's mighty acts of salvation, we praise and adore him, and we are nourished by Word and Sacrament—this is worship. We who are baptized gather each week to give thanks to God and to celebrate the presence and power of his son in our midst.

In worship we are the church. In worship we remember who we are: God's baptized family. In worship we find our identity, our peace, our forgiveness, our meaning, and our mission. Worship is central to our individual lives as Christians, and central also to the life of the whole church.

Christianity is a corporate faith; it is not a private affair between "me and God." We are baptized into the body of Christ, the family of God, the church. Because in Baptism we are joined to God's people, we gather with those people on Sundays to worship, to pray, to hear the Word, and to share in the Eucharist.

Gathering for worship requires a place to gather, and since Old Testament times people have built beautiful buildings to honor God. Almost three thousand years ago, the temple in Jerusalem was dedicated by Solomon. The temple was a place of such splendor that it immediately captured the eye and aroused devotion. The Bible gives exact details of the beauty of the temple. The entire interior was overlaid with pure gold. The doors were carved with cherubim, palm trees, and flowers, and overlaid with gold. A pair of cherubim sixteen feet high, overlaid in gold, were in the Holy of Holies. The temple contained many silver, gold, and bronze lampstands and altars and other furnishings. It was a place of incredible magnificence.

The earliest Christians did not gather for worship in such magnificence. Being a Christian then was a crime. Christians were often under persecution, and discovery led to imprisonment and even death. Christians usually had to worship in secret, and they most often gathered in private homes. That all changed, however, in A.D. 313, when the Roman emperor Constantine declared Christianity a legal religion and brought an end to the persecutions. Since then, Christians have built and dedicated special places for worship. Like the temple in the Old Testament, the early Christian church buildings were often places of great beauty, filled with gold and mosaics and marble. As the number of Christians increased, the need for larger church buildings arose. By the Middle Ages, huge Romanesque and Gothic church buildings were erected across Europe with magnificent stained glass windows, rich sculpture, and other art.

Church buildings are meeting places between God and his people. While God is always and everywhere present, he is present most fully and most powerfully in worship. Worship is the time when we come into God's presence most intentionally and most intensively. Through their architecture and symbolism, church buildings help us to be most fully present to God. Surrounded by reminders of God's awesome and redeeming presence, we worship God, we give him thanks, we praise him for his glory.

Church buildings are places for the people of God to gather for worship, places in which the gospel is proclaimed through Word and Sacrament, places for bringing life and hope to God's people and to the world. The prayer for dedicating a church building makes clear the purposes:

Blessed are you, O Lord our God, king of the universe. The heavens and the earth cannot contain you, yet you are willing to make your home in human hearts. We are the temple of your presence, and this building is the house of your Church. Accept us and this place to which we come to share with others the covenant you make through Holy Baptism, to praise your name, to receive your forgiveness, to hear your Word, and to be nourished by the body and blood of your Son. Be present always to guide and illumine your people. And now, O God, visit us with your mercy and blessing as we dedicate this house to your glory and honor and to the service of all people in the name of the Father, and of the Son, and of the Holy Spirit. Amen

(Occasional Services, p. 169)

It is the privilege of the altar guild to help care for this unique place built and dedicated to the honor and glory of God.

2

The Ministry of
the Altar Guild

Dear Christian friends:
Baptized into the priesthood of Christ,
we are called to offer ourselves
to the Lord of the Church
for what he has done and continues to do for us.

—Occasional Services

These words, from the rite for installing members of the altar guild (see appendix C), point to our motivation for serving in the guild. What has Christ done for us? He died to take away our sin. He rose from the grave to defeat the power of death. He has joined us to his death and resurrection in our Baptism. What does he continue to do for us? He renews in us the power of forgiveness. He gives us hope and joy in the proclamation of the gospel. He gives us love in the fellowship of the church. He gives us the bread of life and the cup of blessing in the Holy Communion. In response to all of this, and to all of God's other mighty acts, we are called to offer ourselves to God's service. The basic motivation for serving in the altar guild—or in any other work of the church—is gratitude.

Members of the altar guild are grateful servants: servants of God, servants of God's people, servants of the liturgy, and servants of the worship space.

Servants of God

Joy is the cardinal attribute of the servants of God. This is the joy of our deliverance from sin and death, the great joy of Christ's incarnation and resurrection. It is the joy of our Baptism, the joy of the gospel, the joy of the Eucharist. Joy stems from our gratitude for all that God has done and is doing for us. More basically, joy is a natural response to God's presence. The joy of these realities enables work in the altar guild to be carried out with a sense of privilege. Whether it is preparing the altar, polishing vessels, removing wax from a linen, arranging flowers, or pressing vestments, the work is never a burden but is always a privilege.

The sense of joy and privilege is coupled with reverence. Reverence is a deep sense of awe and mystery and wonder and ultimate respect in the presence of the Holy One. Our reverence is expressed in the way we speak and act, in how we handle the things of worship and care for the altar, in our attitude toward our fellow servants of the liturgy, and in our own worship and prayer.

Because the altar represents God's presence, it is fitting that we act and speak reverently whenever we are in the worship space. Whether there on Saturday preparing the altar, or on Sunday worshiping with the congregation, conduct should express our devotion to God. When entering the worship space to carry out altar guild responsibilities, it is helpful to pray that the work may be done to the glory of God, and that the tasks may be seen as an opportunity to serve God. A life of prayer is a good and fitting foundation for the work of the altar guild.

Regular corporate worship is also vital for altar guild members. As servants of God, it is important to join others of God's baptized family each Sunday morning. Hearing of the Word and sharing in the Eucharist help us remember who we are and who God is. Worship helps us keep our priorities straight, and provides the context for the work of the altar guild.

We express our joy, reverence, and identity as Christians in various actions as well as with words. Just as God embodied his grace in Jesus, God also made us embodied creatures. We are made of flesh and blood, and God gave us five senses. God relates to us—and we relate to God—in actions as well as words.

Certain actions are filled with meaning for Christians. They symbolize our reverence and our faith; they are enacted prayer. We stand in worship to give honor to the risen Christ who is in our midst. We kneel to express our humility in the presence of God.

Making the sign of the cross is an action that reminds us of our Baptism. Since at least the second century, Christians have made the sign of the cross as a remembrance that in Holy Baptism, God makes us his own children forever. The sign of the cross is a symbol of our salvation, a reminder that on the cross, Christ has consecrated our whole selves—minds, hearts, and actions.

Bowing is also an action of reverence. We may bow our heads in prayer to show our respect for God. We may bow toward the altar, because it represents Christ's presence among us. We may bow toward the cross as it is carried in procession. Many Christians bow when the name of Jesus Christ is mentioned in liturgy, as a sign that we accept him as Lord: "At the name of Jesus every knee should bow, in heaven and on earth and under the earth, and every tongue confess that Jesus Christ is Lord, to the glory of God the Father" (Phil. 2:10–11, *RSV*).

These ritual actions help us embody our faith. They stimulate worshipful and prayerful attitudes. They are a means of expressing and reinforcing our reverence and adoration for the holiness of God. These outward signs of devotion are acceptable to God, for they flow out of hearts full of love for God and obedience to his will. The way we live our lives affects how we serve in the altar guild: "Who can ascend the hill of the Lord and who can stand in his holy place? Those who have clean hands and a pure heart, who have not pledged themselves to falsehood, nor sworn by what is a fraud" (Ps. 24:3–4; *Lutheran Book of Worship*). The inner life of prayer and the corporate life of worship—with confession of sinfulness, praise and adoration of God solely because God is God, thanksgiving for all that God has done for us, petitions for God's help, intercessions for the needs of others, attentive listening to the Word, and faithful sharing in the Supper—are essential for those who serve God in the altar guild.

Servants of God's People

The liturgy is a public event. Corporate worship has both a vertical dimension (involving the worshiper with God) and a horizontal dimension (involving worshipers with each other). Altar guild members are servants of God's people as well as servants of God. This means that guild members will be sensitive to how their work affects other people in the congregation.

People learn about God in part from how God is worshiped. Everything that is done in worship teaches the congregation. The key question is whether what is taught is consistent with the church's theology. If the altar linens and paraments are kept spotless and the eucharistic vessels are beautiful, the congregation learns something of our respect for God. On the other hand, if soiled or wrinkled linens are used, the people may conclude that God is not important enough for careful preparations. It is important for altar guild members to remind themselves continually of the meaning and impact of what they do.

Another responsibility of altar guild members to the congregation is reliability. Corporate worship involves the services of many—altar guild, presiding and assisting ministers, musicians, acolytes, ushers—and it is vital that each person fulfill his or her responsibility. The congregation relies on each person!

Servants of the Liturgy

The liturgy is the church's form of corporate worship. The Sunday liturgy of Word and Sacrament has come to us from our ancestors in the faith, both Jewish and Christian. We use a liturgy derived in part from the ancient synagogue service, consisting of readings, psalms, prayers, and a type of sermon. The other part of our liturgy derives from the Upper Room, when

Jesus identified the bread and wine of the Jewish ritual meal as his body and blood and said, "Do this for the remembrance of me." Since Pentecost, Christians have had an insatiable appetite for this meal, because in it Christ himself is present. We gather for Word and Sacrament because that is what our Lord told us to do. We use a liturgy that has come down to us through the ages because it sets us within the mainstream of Christian worship. This liturgy, from synagogue and Last Supper, helps us remember and celebrate God's mighty acts of salvation.

Members of the altar guild are servants of the liturgy. This ministry involves preparing the worship space with the furnishings, appointments, vessels, elements, linens, and paraments used in the liturgy. As these items are prepared and cared for, it is important that the altar guild understand their meaning and use in worship. Ongoing study is essential. (See chap. 13 for study suggestions.)

Servants of the Worship Space

Altar guild members are also servants of the worship space. Church buildings have been understood in two, sometimes conflicting, ways. In recent decades, the church has often been understood as the house of God, and persons often point to Jacob's words, "This is none other than the house of God, and this is the gate of heaven" (Gen. 28:17). In contrast, the original understanding of the church building was as the house of God's people. The building is the "house of the church," that is, the house of the people who through Baptism comprise the church. This early Christian understanding is now being recovered.

The worship space, however, is really a synthesis of these two concepts. The building is the place of assembly, the place where God's baptized people gather to worship. It is a witness to the corporate nature of the church. The building is also the place of encounter. It is the place where, more intensively than any other place, we encounter the God whose we are; it is also the place where we encounter each other as baptized members of the body of Christ.

Since the worship space is a place where people assemble for encounter with the Holy One, there are several guidelines for that space: beauty, simplicity, quality, worthiness, and appropriateness.

Beauty

Since Old Testament times, people have associated beauty with the worship of God: "Worship the Lord in the beauty of holiness" (Ps. 29:2, *LBW*). Beauty helps set awe and wonder as the context for liturgy. The altar guild has an important responsibility in making the worship space beautiful. Attention is given to the beauty of worship furnishings—beauty in the materials used, their design and form, their color and texture. Another aspect of beauty is harmony—how the various furnishings relate to each other and to the worship space as a whole.

Simplicity

Simplicity is an important part of beauty. The worship space should enable persons' eyes to focus easily and naturally on the central things: altar, font, and pulpit/reading desk. Too many banners, too many flowers and other items make a cluttered space and create visual pollution.

Quality

Quality involves authenticity, as well as the care and skill with which things are made. Phoniness has no place in worship. Everything that is fake or shoddy or of poor quality should be avoided. It is better, for example, to have no flowers at all than to have artificial flowers. Artificial flowers are not real; they are not a part of God's creation. Because they are fake, they simply cannot communicate the beauty of creation.

Worthiness

Worthiness is related to quality. All of the furnishings of the worship space should be worthy of the God whom we worship. They should be the best that the congregation can provide, and they should be cared for well. Soiled linens and wrinkled vestments are not worthy of God or of the worshiping assembly.

The vessels, vestments, paraments, and ornaments of worship should point to the mystery and magnificence of God.

Appropriateness

Things used in worship should be appropriate both to the time of the liturgical year and to the service being used. The worship space should look quite different on a Sunday of Easter from the way it looks, for example, on a Sunday in Advent. Likewise, it should be different for Holy Communion than for Evening Prayer. Things are appropriate when they serve the liturgy; they are inappropriate when they are not in accord with the church's theology and tradition.

3

Worship Space and Appointments

The altar guild is responsible for preparing the settings for the corporate liturgical life of the congregation. The space used for corporate worship is called worship space. Church buildings usually have three main divisions of worship space: narthex, nave, and chancel. It is helpful for members of the altar guild to be familiar with the correct terminology for worship space and its furnishings and appointments.

Narthex

The narthex is the place of entering, a place of transition from everyday life to corporate worship. It is a place for persons to greet one another and to prepare for worship. The narthex also has important liturgical functions. It is used for the formation of liturgical processions prior to the entrance hymn in the liturgy, wedding processions, and the burial procession prior to the funeral liturgy. In addition, the congregation as a whole may gather in or move in procession through the narthex on such days as the Sunday of the Passion (Palm Sunday), Easter Eve, and the Day of Pentecost. Receiving lines after weddings and other services also often form in the narthex.

As a place of entrance, transition, and preparation, the narthex should be an inviting and hospitable place that makes members and visitors feel welcome. It should be kept clean and uncluttered.

Various pieces of art—such as sculpture, wall hangings, and paintings—may be placed in the narthex to reflect the time in the church year. Such art can help worshipers with the transition from the "outside" world to the place and event of corporate worship.

Nave

The nave is the place of assembly, where the congregation gathers for worship. Derived from the Latin word *navis*, which means ship, the nave symbolizes the church sailing in the ocean of time. Congregations are increasingly using chairs rather than pews in the nave, because of the flexibility in seating arrangements that chairs provide. Whether chairs or pews, it is helpful if they have kneelers. It is also useful if the pews or chairs have racks for worship books, Communion registration cards, information cards, and pencils.

Space in the nave needs to be provided for disabled persons—both seating that is easily entered and exited, and open space for wheelchairs.

The aisles are as important as the seats. Aisles have three main functions. First, they allow the people to enter and be seated in the nave. Second, they allow the worshipers access to the altar for the distribution of the Holy Communion. Third, they are the place of processions—entrance processions, gospel processions, offertory processions, wedding processions, burial processions, the procession of light in Evening Prayer, the procession with palms on the Sunday of the Passion, and the procession of the paschal candle at the Easter Vigil. Aisles should be wide enough for easy and safe movement in all of these uses.

Chancel

The third main section of worship space is the chancel, a raised platform in front of the nave. Most worship leadership is conducted from the chancel, since it is the place of both altar and pulpit.

In much traditional architecture, the chancel is composed of two parts: the sanctuary and the choir. The sanctuary is the area immediately surrounding the altar and is usually raised above the level of the rest of the chancel. (The term *sanctuary* is often used erroneously to refer to the entire worship space of a church, but this incorrect usage should be avoided.) Traditionally, the choir is the remaining area of the chancel, but the term is becoming less helpful since the singers are now often seated elsewhere than in the chancel.

The most central furnishing of the chancel is the altar, the table of the Lord. The pulpit or place of the Word is also very important. The third central furnishing of worship space is the font, which is usually not in the chancel itself. (For detailed information about the altar and its appointments, see chap. 7; for the pulpit, see chap. 8; and for the font, see chap. 6.)

Seats for worship leaders may be stalls, pews, or chairs in the chancel. These seats are called sedilia, a Latin word for seats.

The chancel is furnished with various appointments and accouterments that serve both practical and symbolic functions. Some are always used, while the use of others varies with the times of the liturgical year. The visual impact of worship appointments always needs to be considered in their placement, and visual pollution should always be avoided. It is vital never to obscure the central things—altar, pulpit, and font—with secondary and sometimes undesirable items (for example, overly abundant Christmas decorations or floral arrangements). Let the central things *be* central in people's eyes!

Linens and Paraments

Altars have been covered with fine cloths, known as linens, since Old Testament times, and paraments have adorned chancel furnishings since at least the fifth century A.D. While linens are always white, paraments are in fabrics of various colors in order to reflect the liturgical day or season. White is a reminder of the purity and righteousness of the Christ who is unchanging, and it is an expression also of the light and joy Christ gives to his people. Our lives are constantly changing, alternating with joy and sorrow, birth and death—and with the hopeful time of Advent, the joyous days of Christmas, the revelatory time of Epiphany, the preparatory and penitential weeks of Lent, the incomparably celebratory time of Easter, and the weeks of growth after Pentecost. The colors of the paraments reflect these various times and moods, contrasting with the changeless light and love of our Lord. (See chap. 7 for detailed information on linens, and chaps. 7 and 8 for information on paraments.)

Cross

A large cross or crucifix is usually placed near the altar for worship services, though its design and placement may take various forms. The most historic form in liturgical usage is the processional cross, which has been used since the fourth century; "fixed" altar crosses date only from the seventeenth century. Because the cross or crucifix symbolizes Christ's death and resurrection for our redemption, it should be prominent in size and of quality design and construction.

If a processional cross is used, it is carried by its shaft in the entrance procession and placed in a floor standard or wall bracket in the chancel. It is also used for processions outside the church (for example, on the Sunday of the Passion and the Day of Pentecost, or at graveside). The processional cross may also be used for the gospel procession.

Otherwise, a fixed cross may be suspended from the ceiling above the altar or placed on the wall behind the altar. If the altar is not freestanding, the cross stands on the retable.

Candles

Lighted candles are among the oldest ornaments of worship. In ancient times they provided light for reading, but today they usually have only symbolic value. In their most basic sense, candles symbolize Christ as the Light of the world (John 8:12; 12:46).

Two white candles are usually placed on the altar or on floor stands by the altar. They are known as eucharistic lights, although they may be lighted for worship even when the Holy Communion is not celebrated. If the altar is not freestanding, these candles are usually placed on the retable.

Candles for use in worship should be at least 51 percent beeswax so that they will burn evenly and slowly. Candles need to be stored in a cool location. They become harder as they are stored, and thus older candles will burn longer. Electric or battery-powered "candles" are less than authentic and should not be used in the chancel.

Candle followers (sometimes known as caps) placed over the tops of candles will help prevent melted wax from dripping down the sides of the candles, and will also increase the life of the candles.

Candlelighters (also known as tapers) and extinguishers mounted on poles are used by acolytes. The wick in the lighter needs to be kept trimmed, and the extinguishers need regular cleaning to avoid staining linens.

(See chap. 5 for information regarding care of candles and removal of candlewax stains.)

Processional Torches

Torches are large candles placed in wooden or metal shafts which may be carried in procession just behind the processional cross. In design they usually match the processional cross. Processional torches symbolize the coming of Christ to lighten the darkness of the world. They are especially appropriate for festival days, as a way of giving visual emphasis to the festival being celebrated. Torches are placed in floor stands in the chancel, sometimes flanking the altar and sometimes the pulpit. Processional torches have been used to flank  the gospel book for gospel processions since the time of the early church.

Paschal Candle

The paschal candle is a large decorative candle that symbolizes our Lord's glorious Easter triumph over the darkness of death and sin. It is reminiscent of the pillar of cloud and fire that led the people of God to the promised land. Paschal candles have been used in worship since at least the fifth century.

The paschal candle is at least thirty inches tall. It is placed in a decorative floor stand which is usually at least four feet tall. Some great paschal candles in church history weighed three hundred pounds, and some stands were themselves ten feet tall—so important was it to symbolize the magnitude of Christ's Easter victory!

As a part of the Easter Vigil liturgy on Easter Eve, the paschal candle is incised with a cross, the Greek letters *alpha* and *omega*, and the numerals of the current year. The candle is then lighted and carried in procession into the darkened church as the assisting minister sings, "The light of Christ," and the congregation responds, "Thanks be to God." Grains of incense and five wax nails (representing the five wounds of Christ) may be inserted into the cross at the appointed time during the Easter Proclamation in the Vigil. The incense reminds us that behind each nail of the crucifixion is the sweetness of our redemption.

The paschal candle remains in its central position in the chancel throughout the weeks of Easter, and it is lighted for all worship services during the season. On the Day of Pentecost (or on Ascension Day, though Pentecost is preferable to reflect the unity of the great fifty days of Easter), the candle is extinguished by an acolyte as the gospel reading concludes. After that service, the candle is moved to a place near the baptismal font and is lighted for each Baptism. It is a visual connection between Baptism and Easter, reminding us that in our Baptism we are buried and raised with Christ. Small baptismal candles (see chap. 6) are lighted from the paschal candle for presentation to the baptized.

For funerals, the paschal candle is carried immediately behind the processional cross, at the head of the entrance procession. It is placed in its stand at the head of the casket for the burial liturgy.

Sanctuary Lamp

Some churches have a sanctuary lamp in which a candle burns continuously throughout each week of the year. It is suspended from the ceiling or mounted on the chancel wall; it is never properly placed on the altar itself. Sanctuary lamps follow the ancient Jewish custom of always having a light burning at the altar and have come to symbolize God's living presence among us. As such, they are not extinguished following a service.

The altar, however, is a better symbol of God's presence, and the sanctuary lamp is not regarded as essential in the worship life of the Lutheran church. In Roman Catholic and Episcopal churches, the sanctuary lamp signifies the Reserved Sacrament.

Advent Wreath

The Advent wreath, which originated after the Reformation, is a wreath on which four candles are placed, representing the four weeks of waiting during Advent. It is suspended from the chancel ceiling or placed on a stand, usually near the gospel side of the altar (the left side as one faces the altar from the nave). The candles may be blue or purple, or even white. The former practice of three purple candles and one pink candle (which was lighted on Gaudete, the Third Sunday in Advent) no longer reflects our lectionary and calendar.

It is not appropriate to put a so-called Christ candle in the center of the Advent wreath for Christmas (and the paschal candle is *never* properly used for such a purpose)—for the altar candles themselves represent Christ.

Evening Prayer Candle

The Service of Light in Evening Prayer begins with a procession in which a large, lighted candle is carried into the darkened church and placed in its stand in front of the congregation. This candle should be almost as large as the paschal candle, but should be plain white and without decoration. The paschal candle itself is not used for Evening Prayer, because the symbolism and uses of the two candles are quite different. The paschal candle is a resurrection symbol, while the Evening Prayer candle is a reminder of the light of Christ.

Thurible

Also known as a censer, the thurible is a vessel suspended on a chain or chains, which is used for incense, especially in Evening Prayer during Psalm 141 ("Let my prayer rise before you as incense. . ."). The grains of in-  cense are carried in a vessel known as an incense boat, and are sprinkled with a spoon onto lighted charcoal in the thurible. The rising smoke of the incense is a symbol of our prayers ascending to God (see Revelation 8), and its use in Christian worship can be traced back to the fourth century.

Flowers

Since flowers are symbolic of our joy in Christ as well as our human frailty, they are used almost universally to adorn the worship space. However, they are often—and appropriately— omitted during the penitential times of the church year (Lent, Holy Week, and Advent). Only the freshest flowers should be used, and their color and arrangement should be consistent with the season or festival being observed. Because flowers are used for their symbolism of life, joy, and human frailty ("All flesh is grass, and all its beauty is like the flower of the field. The grass withers, the flower fades" Isa. 40:7–8), artificial flowers have no purpose and no place in the worship space.

Potted plants are also not used, because they do not have the same symbolism of sacrifice as cut flowers.

During the growing season, flowers from parishioners' gardens and yards can be arranged for the worship space. Such natural offerings enable the space to be beautified without much expense to the parish.

Flower vases usually coordinate with other worship appointments. Flowers in their vases may be placed in various locations, depending on the design of the worship space. They are not, however, placed on the mensa (the top of the altar), which is reserved for the eucharistic vessels, missal stand, and sometimes candles.

Flowers are usually distributed to the sick and the shut-in at the conclusion of Sunday worship; they are not allowed to remain in the chancel until they wilt or wither. Vases are cleansed and stored after each use; empty vases never remain in the chancel.

Banners

Although they have been used since the sixth century, banners have only recently gained wide popularity. By their nature, banners are meant to be carried in procession and stored after each use, rather than to be placed as fixed or permanent features in the worship space. The purpose of a banner is to employ colors and symbols to represent the day or season being celebrated. The best banners are symbolic and should not have to use words to convey their meaning.

Only well-designed and well-made banners should be used to adorn the place of worship. They should be used sparingly and never in a manner that clutters the space or obscures the central furnishings.

Flags

National flags, being political symbols that mark the divisions of humankind, do not belong in that space where we celebrate our baptismal oneness as citizens in the kingdom of God.

Symbols used in the church should affirm the unity that all peoples can know through Baptism into Christ; national flags are by their nature exclusive.

The so-called Christian flag is unnecessary and superfluous in the space where we focus on the altar and cross or crucifix.

4

Vestments

Vestments are the distinctive garments worn by worship leaders when performing liturgical functions. In various forms vestments have been used since Old Testament times, although Christian vestments are derived largely from garments of the late Roman Empire. Vestments have both utilitarian and symbolic value.

There are several basic purposes for vestments. First, they designate particular liturgical functions. It has been almost universal in human history that people have worn particular clothes for particular functions and particular occasions. For worship leaders, the vestments place less visual emphasis on the person and greater emphasis on the liturgical role being performed, in order that attention and glory may be given to God rather than to the worship leader. Second, in their beauty, vestments reflect and witness to the beauty of God. The beauty of vestments is primarily in their texture, form, and color, rather than in any symbols sewn on them. Third, vestments reflect the continuity of Christian worship through history. Worship leaders today wear essentially the same types of vestments that have been worn since earlier centuries of the Christian church. Thus, vestments provide a visual continuity with our ancestors in the faith.

Clergy Vestments

Alb

The alb is a white ankle-length garment with
close-fitting sleeves. It is the church's oldest vest-
ment. The name comes from the Latin word *albus*,
which means white, and the whiteness symbolizes
the purity and light of Christ. As a vestment, the
alb derives from the white tunic worn by profes-
sional persons in the ancient Roman Empire. Albs
were worn by clergy for all services until the elev-
enth century, when the surplice (see below) began
to be used for noneucharistic worship. Today the
alb is usually worn for all services except Morning
Prayer, Evening Prayer, and Prayer at the Close of the Day
(Compline). When the Holy Communion is celebrated, the
presiding minister usually wears a chasuble over his or her alb.

The alb is gathered at the waist by a cincture, a white rope
or heavy white cord tied at the side. For clergy, the stole is
placed through or tucked under the cincture. An amice, a rectangular neckcloth, has long been worn as a sort of collar with
the alb. The amice originated as a means to protect the alb and
other vestments from perspiration. Some new albs have collars
resembling amices.

Stole

Ordained clergy wear stoles over the alb or surplice
as a sign of their work and their ordination. The stole
is a symbol of the yoke of obedience to Christ (see
Matt. 11:28–30). The stole, being the sign of ordination, is never worn by a lay person.

The stole is a long, narrow band of heavy fabric
worn around the neck. When worn with the alb for
Holy Communion, the stole is crossed over the breast
and tucked under or through the cincture. When worn
over the surplice for other services, the stole hangs
straight in front.

Stoles are worn in the appointed color for the day, and in

fabric and color they usually match the chasuble and paraments.

Chasuble

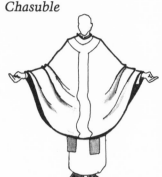

The chasuble is the principal vestment for the presiding minister during the celebration of the Holy Communion. It is a very full vestment worn like a poncho over the alb and stole. The fullness of the chasuble symbolizes the fact that the eucharistic meal is intended to embrace all baptized people; thus, the chasuble is a sign that the abundance of God's grace and the abundance of the eucharistic feast are intended for all God's family.

Chasubles are made of a wide variety of rich fabrics. Their primary symbolism is in their fullness and color, rather than in any symbols attached to them. It is not necessary to put symbols on symbols! The chasuble is often decorated with an orphrey, a strip of contrasting fabric in front and back—either a straight vertical pillar or the shape of a *Y*.

It is ideal for the chasuble to match the stole, as well as the paraments, burse, and chalice veil. The color is that appointed for the day.

Cassock

The cassock is not actually a vestment, but rather is a basic garment over which vestments are worn. Cassocks are black ankle-length garments, which are fitted from the waist up and have narrow sleeves. Cassocks usually button or snap all the way down the front.

For noneucharistic services (especially Morning Prayer, Evening Prayer, and Compline), it is customary for worship leaders to wear cassock and surplice. At eucharistic services the cassock may be worn under the alb.

Surplice

The full-sleeved white vestment worn over the cassock is the surplice. Surplices are at least knee-length, and they derive from the longer and more tailored alb. The whiteness of the surplice symbolizes the purity of Christ.

The surplice is customarily worn over the cassock for Morning Prayer, Evening Prayer, and Prayer at the Close of the Day (Compline).

Surplice

Cope

Cope

The cope is essentially an ornate procession cloak or cape adapted for liturgical use. It is open in the front, fastened near the neck with a clasp known as a morse.

Copes may be worn for festive services of Morning and Evening Prayer, and for ceremonial occasions such as the procession in a wedding, funeral, ordination, installation, or confirmation.

Pectoral Cross

A pectoral cross (from the Latin word *pectus*, which means breast) is a cross on a chain worn by a bishop. It is presented during the bishop's installation as an emblem of the office.

Other Vestments

Lay assisting ministers and acolytes are also appropriately vested for their responsibility in worship leadership. Their vestments are determined by those worn by the presiding minister. That is, if the presiding minister wears an alb, the assisting ministers and acolytes also wear albs. If the presiding minister wears a cassock and surplice, other participating clergy wear cassock and surplice, and lay assisting ministers and acolytes are vested in cassocks and cottas. The cotta is a waist-length version of the surplice. Crucifers usually wear albs.

Choirs, organists, and other musicians usually wear white albs or black cassocks and white cottas; robes resembling academic gowns are to be avoided because of their connotations, and persons who are not ordained do not wear stoles.

Confirmands sometimes wear white capes, which are a reminder of the white baptismal garment. Robes that are academic in style should be avoided, because they give an incorrect and inappropriate connotation to the confirmation rite—it is *not* a graduation, which is what academic garments suggest.

Caring for Vestments

The cleaning, storage, and preparation of vestments are usually the responsibility of the altar guild. Vestments should be kept clean, fresh, and ready to wear at any time, like any other good clothes for special occasions.

Most albs, surplices, and cottas are now made of washable fabrics, and may simply be laundered and pressed. Nonwashable fabrics and all other vestments require dry cleaning by professionals. Most vestments are stored on hangers, but chasubles may be laid flat in large drawers in the sacristy; it is helpful to pad the folds with tissue to avoid creases and possible damage to the fabric.

5

Basic Responsibilities

The altar guild is entrusted with the privilege of preparing the worship space for that gathering of God's family known as corporate worship. This ministry of preparation is as important to the worship life of the church as the pastor's preparation time or the choir's rehearsal. Meaningful worship does not simply happen! It requires reverent and thorough preparation by all who are involved in it. The altar guild is concerned with the things of worship—the care of the worship space, and the care and placement of the furnishings, appointments, and ornaments used in worship. The overall goal of the altar guild is to see that the worship space is kept beautiful and in good order, both to glorify God and to provide a setting that helps enable the congregation to worship in a meaningful way. It is also the responsibility of the altar guild to keep the worship space ready for persons' individual use for prayer between services.

Members of the altar guild are servants of the liturgy, and they have several basic responsibilities. Housekeeping is one of the basic tasks, and it is best carried out with the attitude that it is a high privilege to care for the things that symbolize God's love and presence. The altar guild, along with the sexton, is responsible for keeping the chancel, altar, font, and pulpit clean and free of clutter. Linens, paraments, and vestments are cleaned regularly and kept pressed in readiness for use in worship. The sacramental vessels and other worship appointments are kept clean and polished. Adequate supplies of bread, wine, candles, and other necessities are secured and properly stored.

All of this work should be done with a full understanding of the meaning and significance of the items being handled. Members of the guild should know the names of the furnishings and accouterments as a means of respect and reverence and to increase their efficiency. This learning, in turn, will help make worship itself more meaningful for guild members.

The Sacristy

Sacristies are small rooms, usually just off the chancel, which are used for worship preparation and storage. Most congregations will want to provide two sacristies. One is the pastor's sacristy, a private room in which vestments are kept and where the worship leaders vest and have devotions before the liturgy. The pastor's sacristy should have a sink (with soap and hand towels) and a full-length mirror. An attached restroom is useful.

The second is the working sacristy, which functions as the headquarters of the altar guild. Here are kept paraments, linens, sacramental vessels and supplies, candles and candle stands, flower vases, altar book and missal stand, funeral palls, hymn board numbers, oil for anointing, baptismal garments, thurible and incense, and other items needed for worship. The sacramental vessels and other items made of precious metal are usually kept in locked cabinets or a safe. The wine is also usually stored in a locked cabinet, or in a locked refrigerator.

In the working sacristy are also kept other needed items: iron, ironing board, dustcloths and other cleaning supplies, stain removal supplies, polishes, scissors, matches, sewing supplies, tools for flower arranging, and so forth. It is helpful if the sacristy has a bulletin board and a church year calendar. The sacristy also needs a sink and a piscina—a sink with a drain which goes directly into the ground for disposing of baptismal water (if water is not kept in the font) and wine remaining in the chalice (if it is not consumed by the ministers after the sacramental celebration).

In addition to storage, the working sacristy is also used for such tasks as cleaning sacramental vessels, polishing worship ornaments, arranging flowers, trimming candles, and mending paraments and vestments. Adequate counter space in the sacristy is important.

Routine Preparations

Certain routine preparations are done prior to any worship service (whether it is a Sunday morning liturgy, a funeral, a wedding, or another special service). Basic procedures before services include at least the following:

1. Clean the chancel and see that all furnishings and appointments are dusted, polished, and in their proper places. Remove any items that will not be used.
2. Clean and press the needed linens and paraments, and put them in place. Be sure that the paraments are of the designated liturgical color for the day by consulting the church year calendar and appendix A at the back of this book.
3. If it will be used, place the altar book on its stand and mark the propers according to directions from the presiding minister.
4. If there will be flowers, arrange them and put them in place.
5. Make sure that the candles are in place, with wicks upright and ready to be lighted. Check the candlelighter (taper) to be sure there is adequate wick and that the wick is trimmed, and clean the extinguisher of soot and wax if necessary. Provide matches for the acolytes.
6. Place correct numbers on hymn boards.
7. Put bulletins in place for ministers and acolytes.
8. Be sure that vestments for the presiding minister, assisting ministers, and acolytes are clean and pressed.
9. For celebrations of Holy Communion or Holy Baptism,

prepare the sacramental vessels, linens, and elements.
(See chaps. 6, 7, and 8.)

10. If a processional cross, processional torches, or banners
    are to be used, be sure their stands are in place.

Other responsibilities of preparation for particular services
and days are listed in chapters 9–11.

After Worship

There are also routine procedures to be carried out after each
service, in order to prepare the church as a place for prayer until
the next corporate service. Sacramental vessels, flowers, flower
vases, altar book, missal stand, processional cross and torches
are removed from the chancel. The flowers are prepared for distribution to the sick and shut-in. The other items are kept in
the sacristy until the next service. Empty vases and the missal
stand are never left on the altar or in the chancel when not in
use. Soiled linens and paraments are removed and cleaned. Any
other items left in the chancel (such as bulletins, tissues, and
worship books) are removed. Candle wicks are pulled into an
upright position. Other responsibilities following Holy Communion and Holy Baptism are listed in chapters 6 and 7.

If the church building is open during the week for prayer,
paraments should be changed according to the calendar.

Cleaning and Stain Removal

Linens

Linens for Holy Communion and Holy Baptism should be
laundered and ironed after each use. The fair linen and credence linen should be laundered at least monthly and whenever they become soiled or spotted. Dusty, stained, or wrinkled
linens have no place on the table of the Lord!

Laundering the linens is the responsibility of altar guild
members. These linens are not usually sent to commercial
cleaners. They should be laundered in separate loads in the
washing machine's gentle cycle, or by hand. A mild unscented
soap is used. Bleach, blueing, and starch are avoided, since the

chlorine in bleach and some detergents is likely to damage fine fabrics. Several rinsings are helpful, and white vinegar in the final rinse cycle will help remove soap and minerals in the water.

The sooner stains are treated, the easier they are to remove. Lipstick stains on purificators and wine stains on various linens can usually be removed by carefully rubbing mild liquid detergent on the stain; repeat the procedure if necessary. For more stubborn wine stains, sprinkle with table salt, and pour boiling water through them until the stains disappear.

Blood stains should be soaked in cold water and then laundered. Diluted ammonia will help remove dried blood stains.

Wax drippings on linens may be removed by scraping with a blunt instrument such as the back of a knife. Then place a white blotter or absorbent brown wrapping paper under the linen, and press over the spot with a moderately hot iron until the wax is absorbed by the paper. Remove the residual stain with alcohol or lemon juice, and then launder the linen. Black wax spots can be prevented by keeping the candle extinguishers clean.

After laundering, linens should not be wrung, but rolled in towels to remove excess water. Linens are ironed while still quite damp, first on the wrong side and then the right side. It is important that they be perfectly dry before being rolled or folded for storage, or they will be uneven and rippled, and they could mildew. Folds are made by hand after pressing, not with the iron itself.

Fair linens, protector linens, and credence linens are stored rolled on heavy tubes and wrapped in acid-free tissue paper. Other linens may be laid flat in clean drawers, or folded.

Paraments

Paraments need to be cleaned less frequently than linens, but they require dry cleaning by experts. Instructions for such cleaning may come with the paraments and should be retained for reference. Paraments should be inspected weekly for soiling and ought always to be spotless.

Candlewax can be removed from some paraments by the blotting paper and ironing method described above for linens. However, care is needed, and it may be best to consult an expert dry cleaner.

Paraments may be stored flat in clean drawers, or by hanging over rods in special cabinets. Paraments should never be folded, since this eventually causes the fabric to warp and deteriorate.

Carpet

Wax drippings on carpets can be prevented most of the time by using followers (caps) on the candles. When they do occur, however, place blotting paper on top of the wax, and press over it, repeating the procedure until the wax is absorbed.

Candles and Candleholders

Candles and candleholders require special care because of the wax drippings. If candle followers (caps) are used, they need to be removed and cleaned periodically. Remove them from the candles while the wax is still warm. Hardened wax can be removed from candle followers and candleholders (except those made of lacquered metals) by rinsing or soaking them in very hot water and wiping them with paper towels. Be careful, however, to avoid pouring the waxy water down the drain. Scraping the hardened wax with a knife or fingernails is not recommended, since it may scratch the finish. For candleholders made of lacquered metals, soften the wax with hot air from a hairdryer, and wipe off with a paper towel.

Wax drippings down the sides of the candles themselves may be peeled off when the wax has become completely cold. The candles should be held in a clean cloth or with cotton gloves in order to prevent finger marks. Candles can be cleaned with some alcohol or salad oil on a soft cloth.

The soot and wax on candle extinguishers can be removed with very hot water and paper towels.

Other Furnishings and Appointments

All of the furnishings and ornaments used in worship should be handled reverently and cleaned carefully. In general, it is wise to wear soft cotton gloves when handling these items, since the moisture and oils of the skin will tarnish many metals and may mark candles.

Altar appointments and other worship ornaments are found in a variety of metals and other materials. The best policy is to obtain detailed instructions for their care and cleaning from the manufacturer. If this is not possible, certain general guidelines may be helpful.

Items made of brass may or may not be lacquered to prevent tarnishing. If they are lacquered, they should be wiped clean with a soft damp cloth and dried immediately with a clean soft cloth. Under no circumstances should lacquered brass be immersed in water, touched with detergents or abrasives, or polished; such procedures will damage the lacquer. When the lacquer begins to wear or peel, the item should be relacquered by a jeweler or the manufacturer.

Brass appointments that are not lacquered should be cleaned and polished frequently with a soft cloth and a fine grade of metal polish. Unlacquered brass must never be touched with bare hands or damp cloths, since these cause tarnishing.

Silver appointments should be washed in hot soapy water, rinsed in clear hot water, dried immediately, and polished with a good grade of silver polish. Never allow polish to dry on the surface.

When not in use, these appointments should be stored in clean cotton flannel bags to prevent tarnishing. Each item should have its place in the sacristy, with everything labeled to prevent unnecessary handling.

6

Holy Baptism: Place and Preparation

The three foci of worship space relate to the three major actions of corporate worship: the celebration of Holy Baptism (Christians are people "in the water" with our Lord), the proclamation of the Word of God (we are people who stand before the book of life), and the celebration of the Holy Communion (we are people who gather at the table of the Lord).

Holy Baptism is our entrance into the church of Christ; it is the rite of Christian initiation into the family of God. Both historically and theologically, there is a significant connection between Baptism and Easter, because Baptism is a ritual but very real sharing of the death and resurrection of our Lord. As Saint Paul wrote; "When we were baptized in Christ Jesus, we were baptized into his death. We were buried therefore with him by Baptism into death, so that as Christ was raised from the dead by the glory of the Father, we too might live a new life. For if we have been united with him in a death like his, we shall certainly be united with him in a resurrection like his" (Rom. 6:3–5). Baptism is our radically significant participation in the events of Good Friday and Easter, our threshold between death and life. It is the most important and most consequential event in our lives.

The way in which a parish celebrates Holy Baptism can emphasize the meaning and importance of this sacrament for a person's life—or, at worst, it can allow Baptism to appear to be a merely perfunctory or sentimental act.

The altar guild's first responsibility in preparing for the celebration of Baptism is to study the meaning of this sacrament. A clear understanding of the baptismal liturgy and an appreciation of the symbolic meaning of the items used will help Baptism recover its central place in the Christian life.

During much of the history of the Christian church, Baptism was celebrated only on Easter Eve, at the Easter Vigil. Such a practice underscores the central relationship between Baptism and Easter. To restore Holy Baptism to its rightful place in the life of the church, many congregations are again celebrating Baptism at the Easter Vigil, as well as on the Day of Pentecost, All Saints' Day, and the Baptism of Our Lord (First Sunday after the Epiphany). Baptismal festivals on these occasions help keep Baptism integrated into the unfolding story of salvation provided in the liturgical year. If your congregation observes such baptismal festivals, the altar guild may need to make preparations for the Baptism of several persons.

The Water

Water is the earthly element used for Baptism. Water is an agent of both creation and destruction, both life and death, both birth and drowning. Throughout the Bible, water is a powerful image of God's saving acts. God created both land and water, and with water continues to nourish and sustain all living things. The waters of the flood destroyed the wicked and saved Noah and his family. Israel was led through the sea out of slavery into the freedom of the promised land. Jesus was baptized in the waters of the Jordan River, and later he used water to wash his disciples' feet. He made water a sign of cleansing and rebirth, a sign of the kingdom of God.

In the waters of Baptism, we are buried with our Lord. Our sinfulness, an otherwise ultimate destiny of eternal death, and the chaos of our lives are drowned in the waters of the font. We are raised up out of the water to share in the new life in Christ. Baptism is the most important event in our lives.

The Font

Water, of course, always needs a container. For Holy Baptism, that container is the baptismal font. The font is, at once, the tomb in which we are buried, the womb in which we are reborn, and the pool in which we are bathed.

Through much of church history, the size and shape of the font reflected the meaning of Baptism. Fonts in the fifth and sixth centuries, for example, were pools as large as twenty-five feet in diameter, to accommodate the immersion of several persons. Often they were hexagonal (six-sided) to symbolize the sixth day of the week as the day of Christ's crucifixion, or octagonal (eight-sided) to symbolize Sunday, the "eighth day," as the day of resurrection. Unfortunately, there has been a trend through the centuries to minimize the size of the font, with a resulting decrease in people's understanding of the significant meaning of Baptism. Today many congregations are reversing that trend, realizing that the size and shape of the font help people recognize what Baptism means for their lives. As the *Lutheran Book of Worship* expresses it, "In Holy Baptism our gracious heavenly Father liberates us from sin and death by joining us to the death and resurrection of our Lord Jesus Christ."

Fonts are constructed of a variety of materials in several shapes. The most appropriate fonts are large enough at least to

allow for the immersion of infants, and some fonts are adequate for the immersion of adults. Hexagonal, octagonal, or cruciform (shaped like a cross) fonts probably best symbolize the meaning of the sacrament.

Some fonts have covers, although they are no longer necessary. Font covers originated in medieval times when the consecrated water was believed to have magical powers. There were instances when people stole the water for magical purposes, so churches were required to keep the fonts covered and locked. Today it is unlikely that people will steal water from the font, and therefore font covers are superfluous. It is better to keep water in the font and to allow people to see it and be reminded of their Baptism.

The location of the baptismal font varies. There are, however, two guidelines. First, the location should suggest Baptism as entrance into the family of God—and thus a location just inside the nave, perhaps in the center aisle, is meaningful. Second, the space around the font should be adequate for several persons to gather around it for the sacrament. There should also be space for the paschal candle, and it is helpful if there is a small table or shelf nearby for the ewer (if needed), baptismal garment, baptismal candle, towel, and oil.

It is ideal for the font to have running water and a drain. If it does not, water is carried to the font in a large pitcher known as a ewer.

Other Items

Oil

Following the washing with water in Baptism, the rite suggests that the sign of the cross be made with oil on the forehead of the baptized. This practice has been followed since the second century, but it derives from an Old Testament practice of putting a mark on the foreheads of persons whom God would save. The cross is a tangible reminder that in Baptism we are united with the crucified Christ and sealed by the Holy Spirit. Olive oil is usually used for this purpose, both because it is easily absorbed by the skin, and because the olive tree is a traditional symbol of peace and reconciliation. The oil is known as chrism (from the same Greek word from which the title "Christ" is derived, referring to the "Anointed One"). The olive oil is usually mixed with a fragrant oil such as balsam, because the fragrance is a sign of joy and gladness and also because it helps keep the oil from smelling rancid. Prepared chrism as well as fragrant oils which can be mixed with olive oil are available from ecclesiastical suppliers.

Chrism is usually kept in a small vessel for this purpose, known as a stock. The stock holds a piece of cotton, which is saturated with chrism. If an oil stock is not available, the chrism may be placed in a small cruet or shallow bowl.

Paschal Candle and Baptismal Candles

To emphasize the relationship between Baptism and the death and resurrection of our Lord, it is traditional to place the paschal candle near the font (except during the weeks of Easter, when it is placed in a prominent location in the chancel) and to light it whenever there is a Baptism.

In many congregations a small white candle is lighted from the paschal candle during the baptismal liturgy and presented to the newly baptized person (or parent or sponsor), to be lighted on each baptismal anniversary. Just as we honor physical birth by lighting candles on birthday cakes, baptismal candles can help us honor our spiritual rebirth in Holy Baptism. Lighting the baptismal candle from the paschal candle (rather than from altar candles) helps reinforce the important connection between Baptism and Easter.

Baptismal Garment

A white baptismal garment may be presented to the newly baptized by a representative of the congregation. Known as a chrisom, the white garment is a visible reminder that in Baptism we are clothed in the righteousness of Christ. The baptismal garment is also a symbol of the eternal life that begins in the font, a symbolism echoed by the white pall placed over a casket for the burial liturgy.

The garment may be quite simple, made by a member of the altar guild or someone else in the parish. For an infant, it may be a rectangular white cloth with a center opening for the baby's head. For older persons, a poncho-style white garment may be sewn. The baptismal garment should not resemble an academic gown.

Preparations for Baptism

If water is not kept in the font at all times, it needs to be placed in the ewer and put near the font before the service in which the Baptism is to occur. The font and ewer should be cleaned and polished prior to each Baptism.

Other items also need to be provided near the font: a baptismal towel, white baptismal garment, and baptismal candle for each candidate. If a baptismal shell is used, it is laid on top of the towel. If anointing with oil is to occur, the oil in the stock is placed near the font, and a purificator should also be provided for wiping the presiding minister's hand.

After Baptism, if water is not kept in the font, it may be poured on the ground or into a piscina (a special drain which connects directly to the ground).

7

Holy Communion:
Place and Preparation

The Holy Communion is the chief service of the church. It is known by many names, including the Eucharist, the Sacrament of the Altar, and the Lord's Supper. By whatever name, this sacrament is the feast of the baptized family of God, gathered around the table of the Lord. In Holy Baptism we are initiated into God's family; in Holy Communion we are sustained in that family. In Holy Baptism we are made part of the priesthood of all believers; in Holy Communion we are nourished and strengthened to carry out our priesthood of witness and service in the world. In Holy Baptism we are joined to our Lord's death and resurrection; in Holy Communion we both proclaim his death and celebrate the feast of his victory.

The altar guild has a special and privileged responsibility to prepare for this celebration which is so central to Christian worship. It is important for guild members to grow continually in the meaning of the Eucharist, as well to be thoroughly familiar with the names and use of eucharistic vessels and linens.

The Altar

The focal point of the worship space is the altar, the table of the Lord. More than any other furnishing, the altar symbolizes God's constant presence in his church. The altar is therefore the center of the church's life, both architecturally and liturgically.

The term altar is derived from the Latin word *alta*, which means high. The altar is usually on a raised platform known as a predella. Its height both enhances the dignity and the significance of the altar, and enables the assembled congregation to see the actions at the altar.

The altar is the table for the Holy Communion meal—the place where the eucharistic feast is celebrated and around which God's baptized family gathers to share this feast. In the early church the altar was free-standing, and the presiding minister faced the people for the eucharistic celebration. During later centuries when theology began to deteriorate, people were often considered unworthy to commune. The altar was moved against the east wall of the church, often far away from the congregation. The priest celebrated the Eucharist with his back to the people.

Luther and the Reformation helped restore the Holy Communion to the people, and finally we are again seeing altars placed in a free-standing position as tables. In this position, the ministers stand behind the altar for the Great Thanksgiving in the Holy Communion liturgy, facing the people in a more courteous, hospitable, and intimate relationship. The free-standing altar witnesses to the meal character and fellowship of the Eucharist.

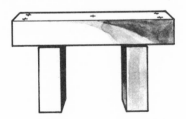

The top of the altar is known as the mensa, which means table. The height of the mensa is thirty-nine inches, and it is usually rectangular or square. Five Greek crosses are inscribed into the top of the mensa, one at each corner and one in the center. The crosses represent the five wounds of our crucified Lord.

The mensa is used only as the table for the eucharistic feast.

Nothing is placed on it except altar linens, the missal stand, eucharistic vessels, and sometimes candles.

Altars which are not free-standing often have a retable, which is a small shelf above the back of the mensa. On the retable (which is sometimes also called a gradine) may be placed the altar cross, flower vases, and candles. Flower vases are not placed on the mensa itself.

Older churches often have a reredos, which is a high extension of the retable, made of carved wood or stone. When there is no reredos, an ornamental cloth known as a dossal is sometimes used as background for an altar which is not free-standing.

Altar Linens

Three linens are traditionally used to vest the altar, marking it as the table of the Lord. They are on the altar at all times, except that they are removed at the conclusion of the Maundy Thursday liturgy, and the altar remains bare on Good Friday.

Cerecloth

The first linen placed on the mensa (the top of the altar) is the cerecloth. When the altar is stone, the cerecloth is waxed or otherwise waterproofed to prevent dampness from staining the other linens and from damaging the various vessels. Otherwise it is simply a heavy linen and helps protect the mensa. The cerecloth measures the exact dimensions of the top of the mensa.

When the cerecloth is removed from the altar, it is rolled carefully in order to prevent wrinkles, which in a waxed fabric may be impossible to remove.

Protector Linen

Over the cerecloth is often placed a second linen, to which the altar parament(s) may be sewn. This protector linen is the same depth as the mensa and the same width as the parament.

Fair Linen

The fair linen is the most important of the altar linens, because it represents the burial linen or shroud in which our

Lord's body was wrapped after his crucifixion. The word *fair* refers to the fine quality and cleanliness of this linen. Thus, because of its symbolism and because it is very visible to the worshiping assembly, the fair linen should always be spotless and fresh. Each church will find it necessary to own at least two fair linens, so that one is always clean and ready to use. When laundered, the fair linen is never folded.

The fair linen is the same depth as the top of the mensa, but its length may vary, depending on the altar and its paraments. Often the fair linen extends over the ends of the mensa one-third or two-thirds the height of the altar, or it may be the same length as the mensa. Generous hems (as much as two inches) help the fair linen hang straight and lie flat.

Traditionally, five Greek crosses are embroidered in white on the fair linen—one in the center, and one near each corner of the mensa. The five crosses symbolize the five wounds of Christ.

It is not appropriate to place lace edges on the fair linen.

Sacramental Linens

Four additional linens are used for the celebration of the Holy Communion: the corporal, the pall, purificators, and the veil. These linens are carried in a burse.

Corporal

The corporal is a square of fine linen which is laid by an assisting minister on the center of the altar over the fair linen during the offertory. The eucharistic vessels are then set on the corporal. This linen is sometimes interpreted to symbolize the linen placed over the face of Christ for his burial. The corporal is one of the most ancient altar linens used for Christian worship.

Depending on the depth of the altar, the corporal is usually about twenty inches square. A small Greek cross is usually embroidered in white near the center front edge.

The corporal is folded and ironed inside out in thirds each way (forming nine squares), so that it can be unfolded on the altar with the right side up. Thus, when it is refolded as the altar is cleared, crumbs of bread are folded into it and not dropped onto the mensa or the floor. It is carried to and from the altar in the burse. A fresh corporal is used for each celebration of the Eucharist, and each congregation needs several corporals.

Pall

Used to cover the chalice before and after Communion, the pall is a linen-covered square of stiff cardboard, aluminum, or plastic. The size of the pall is determined by the diameter of the chalice, but it is usually six to nine inches square. The top of the pall is often embroidered in white with a cross or a symbol relating to the church year.

The linen covering the pall is usually sewn as a pocket, so that the stiff lining may be removed for laundering the linen. A clean pall should always be used.

Purificators

Purificators are square linen napkins used to wipe the rim of the chalice during the distribution. The size depends on the size of the chalice, since the purificator is draped over the chalice before and after the celebration, but the size is often twelve to fifteen inches square. It is folded like the corporal, except right side out.

Several purificators are needed for each chalice for each eucharistic service. When not in use, they are kept in the burse.

Veil

Several kinds of veils may be used. The chalice veil matches the paraments and vestments in the color for the day; when this veil is used, the burse matches the veil in color and fabric.

When a whole loaf of bread is used for the Eucharist, a white linen veil—perhaps a second corporal or a large purificator—is sometimes used to cover it prior to the offertory.

Some congregations use a large white linen veil as a post-Communion cover for the vessels and elements.

Burse

Sacramental linens are carried to and from the altar in the burse, which is an envelopelike case. The burse matches the chalice veil, paraments, stole, and chasuble in the liturgical color for the day. It is constructed with two squares of cardboard, about nine inches square, each covered with linen and bound together on one side. This is covered with another piece of fabric, matching the paraments, so that the sides are pleated like bellows.

Congregations using chalice veils and burses will need a set in each liturgical color.

Paraments

Paraments adorn the altar in the appointed colors of the liturgical day or season, helping to make the altar the visual focus of the worship space. In pointing to the day or season through colors and symbols, paraments serve also devotional and educational functions. Paraments have been used since at least the fifth century A.D.

There are five types of altar paraments in use: the frontal, the Laudean frontal, the superfrontal, the antependium, and the frontlet. The type selected for a specific altar is influenced by the style of the altar, and may also vary according to the time of the church year.

A frontal covers the entire front of the altar, from the front top edge of the mensa down to the predella. This type of frontal

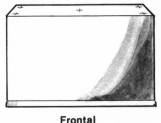

Frontal

Laudean Frontal

may be attached to the protector linen, which is covered with the fair linen.

A Laudean frontal (sometimes known as a Jacobean frontal)

covers the entire altar, hanging to the predella on all four sides of a freestanding altar or the sides and front of an east-wall altar.

A superfrontal may be used alone or as a part of the frontal. It covers the length of the altar, but hangs down only ten to twelve inches from the top of the mensa.

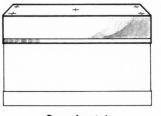

Superfrontal

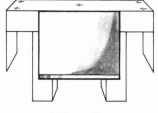

Antependium

An antependium, much narrower than a frontal, covers one-third to one-half the front of the altar. It may hang all the way to the floor, but usually is made to extend over the front of the altar about three-fourths the height of the altar. It is hung in the center of the altar.

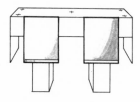

Frontlets

Frontlets are hung down the front of the altar in pairs. They are usually two to three feet wide and extend about two-thirds of the distance to the predella.

Colors

Congregations will find it useful to provide at least eight sets of paraments and vestments to accommodate the colors of the church year.

White is the color of light, gladness, purity, and joy in Christ. White is thus the liturgical color appointed for festivals of

Christ—the Annunciation, the Visitation, Christmas and its season, the Name of Jesus, the Epiphany, the Baptism of Our Lord, the Presentation, the Transfiguration, the ˙Sundays of Easter (although gold is an alternate color for Easter Day itself), and Christ the King. White is also used for certain other festivals (such as the Holy Trinity) and commemorations, and it is the alternate color for Maundy Thursday. If seasonal symbols appear on paraments, it may be wise to have more than one white set, in order to relate each more closely to the varying times of the church year.

Bright red is the color of fire—the fire of the Holy Spirit. Red is used for the Day of Pentecost, for martyrs' days, and for certain other days celebrating events in the church, such as Reformation, ordination, and church dedications and anniversaries.

Scarlet is a hue deeper than red; scarlet is the color of blood. It is used during Holy Week—from the Sunday of the Passion (Palm Sunday) through Maundy Thursday. The color should be selected carefully so it is not confused with the bright red used for festivals.

Purple is the penitential color of Lent. It is also the alternate color for Advent, when it is interpreted as the royal color of the coming King. In congregations where purple is used for both Lent and Advent, it will be helpful to have two different sets, with appropriate and distinctive symbols on each.

Blue is the preferred color for Advent, because it is the color of hope, a central theme of Advent. Pale and navy blues should be avoided, in favor of royal blue.

Green is the color of growth, and it is used during the seasons after Epiphany and Pentecost.

Gold is the appropriate alternate color for Easter Day, since that day is the "queen of feasts," the most important day in the church year. The use of gold paraments on that one day helps to distinguish it in a special visual way from the remainder of the year.

Black, the color of ashes and humiliation and mourning, is appointed for Ash Wednesday.

Missal Stand and Altar Book

The missal stand holds the large service book (*Lutheran Book of Worship Ministers Edition*). It may be a wood or metal bookstand, or simply be a cushion on which the service book rests for the celebration of the Eucharist. The missal stand and altar book should be removed when not in use.

Eucharistic Vessels

Vessels used for the celebration of the Holy Communion usually constitute a matched set of fine metal such as silver or gold. Pewter or earthenware vessels may also be used. The appearance and material of the vessels should be worthy of the precious elements they hold—containers appropriate for the body and blood of our Lord. A minimum set of eucharistic vessels includes a chalice, paten, and flagon or cruet. If hosts (rather than a whole loaf of bread) are used, a ciborium or host box is also needed.

 The chalice is the large cup used for the consecration and distribution of the sacramental wine. The cup portion of the chalice is attached to the base (or foot) by the stem. If the distribution is not by common cup, the chalice needs a pouring lip. In this situation, the wine is poured from the chalice into a small glass held by the communicant. Prefilled individual glasses should *never* be used. Increasingly, congregations are returning to the traditional common cup, because it is a fuller symbol of the unity we share in Christ.

The paten is the plate used for the sacramental bread. Its size depends on the type of bread used. It is traditional prac-  tice for the paten to be set on the rim of the chalice for vesting in veil and burse. When a whole loaf of bread is used, however, another larger paten or basket is usually also needed.

A flagon or cruet is usually used to hold the wine before it is poured into the chalice. The flagon is a tall covered pitcher, usually made of fine metal. The cruet is a glass vessel with a stopper, often topped with a cross.

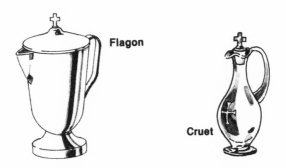

Flagon

Cruet

When hosts (wafers) rather than a loaf of bread are used, they are kept in a ciborium or host box. A ciborium is similar to a chalice, but has a fitted lid. A host box (also known as a pyx) is a short round container with a lid.

Ciborium

Host Box

In some congregations the presiding minister ritually cleanses his or her hands prior to the Great Thanksgiving. For this, a small dish known as a lavabo bowl is used. The water is poured over the hands from a cruet, and the hands are dried with a lavabo towel. This is a small linen towel, usually twelve by eighteen inches. It is folded lengthwise, right side out, in thirds, so that it will hang evenly over the arm of the assisting minister or acolyte.

A spoon is sometimes useful for removing foreign particles from the wine in a chalice. The bowl of a spoon made for this purpose is perforated.

The Elements

At the Last Supper, our Lord took bread and wine, gave thanks to God, and declared that they were his body and blood! He shared the bread and wine with his disciples, and told them to "Do this for the remembrance" of him. After his crucifixion and resurrection, he revealed himself to two of his disciples on the Emmaus road in the breaking of bread. Christ's followers of all times have had an insatiable appetite for this bread and wine, because they know that in them the Lord himself is present. When the prayer and actions of the Upper Room are repeated by the presiding minister, we share the very life of the crucified and risen Christ. The Lord is truly present "in, with, and under" the bread and the wine in the Holy Communion.

Bread signifies several things biblically and in our own time. The ancient Israelites believed that bread came from the hands of God—and indeed, in the Eucharist, it does. Bread also carries the image of death and resurrection: the wheat seed is buried in the earth, where it comes to life and sprouts; and then the grain is crushed to be harvested so that flour can be made and bread can rise. Bread also, of course, satisfies basic human hunger.

The early Christian church always used ordinary bread for Holy Communion, a practice that is still preferred. A whole loaf of bread has advantages over individual wafers, because the one loaf is a powerful symbol of our unity in Christ: "When we break the bread, is it not a means of sharing in the body of Christ? Because there is one loaf, we, many as we are, are one body; for it is one loaf of which we all partake" (1 Cor. 10:16–17, NEB). The breaking and sharing of the bread is a symbol also of our Lord's crucifixion, a witness to his own body being broken on the tree of the cross.

Carefully made homemade wheat bread is particularly good for the Eucharist, for its visual reminder that God takes common earthly elements and human labor and uses them for his extraordinary purposes. Bread that crumbles easily should be avoided. When a whole loaf of bread is used, provision should be made for cleaning the chancel after the service. Several sacramental bread recipes are provided later in this chapter.

Wine is used for the Holy Communion because that is what Christ used in the Upper Room and directed us to use when we celebrate his holy meal. In addition, wine is used because of its unique meaning. While Psalm 104 speaks of bread for strength, it speaks of wine for gladdening our hearts. Bread was a staple in ancient Jewish meals, but wine was used only for festive occasions. The purpose of wine was not to quench thirst, but to give joy and life. Thus, wine is not only the blood of Christ by its institution by him; it is also a sign of the festive and joyful nature of the eucharistic meal. Grape juice, which is artificial wine, is not appropriate for this sacramental feast.

The wine may be homemade, purchased commercially, or purchased from an ecclesiastical supplier. A fine dinner wine should be used, avoiding sweet port. Only wine made from grapes should be used. The wine may be white or red. Red, however, is more difficult to remove from linens.

The Credence and Offertory Table

The credence is a small shelf or table near the altar on which the eucharistic vessels and missal stand are kept prior to the offering. Many churches have two credences—one for the sacramental vessels and one for the offering plates and alms basins.

The offertory table is a small table near the rear of the nave where the bread and wine are placed until they are carried forward, along with the money offering, during the offertory.

Both the credence and offertory tables are covered with white linen cloths.

Setting the Table of the Lord

Preparation of the altar for the eucharistic feast should be done well ahead of the celebration. The first tasks are to be certain that the chancel and its furnishings are clean, that unnecessary items are removed, that the correct paraments are in place, that all linens are freshly laundered and ironed, that all of the sacramental vessels are clean and polished, and that sufficient quantities of bread and wine are ready.

Most important in all of the preparatory work is that it be done with the reverence and good order that befit Christ's presence. Awareness of Christ's presence in the sacrament will ensure that the work is done with genuine joy and gratitude for God's grace. To prepare the Lord's table is an immense privilege!

There are various acceptable ways of arranging the vessels for the Eucharist. The method used in a given parish will be determined by the available chancel furnishings and vessels, by the pastor's preferences, and by a sense of good liturgical order.

In determining parish customs, the altar guild and the pastor must first ascertain the resources of the church. Is the credence to be used? Is the altar free-standing? Are burse and veil to be used? Is the paten a proper size to fit into the rim of the chalice? Is there an offertory procession? Is the pastor right- or left-handed? Are there assisting ministers? Answers to questions such as these will help in selecting a method for preparing the table of the Lord.

The chalice is often vested in the traditional manner. It is done in several steps:

1. A purificator folded in thirds lengthwise is placed over the mouth of the empty chalice, so that the right and left sides hang evenly over the edges of the chalice.
2. The paten is placed on top of the purificator. (If hosts rather than whole loaf are to be used, a large host may be placed on the paten.)
3. The paten is covered with the pall.

- 1 -   - 2 -   - 3 -

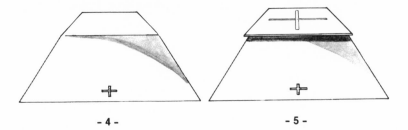

- 4 -   - 5 -

4. The chalice veil in the proper color of the day is placed over the pall and arranged so that a trapezoid is seen when viewed from the front.

5. The corporal and additional purificators are placed in the burse, which matches the veil. The burse is laid on top of the vested chalice.

It is preferable for the vested chalice (as well as flagon and other vessels) to be kept on a credence until the offering, at which time an assisting minister carries it to the altar and sets the table. However, if there is no credence, the vested chalice may be set on the altar prior to the service.

During the offering, the corporal is placed on the altar, and the vessels are set on the corporal. The following arrangement is appropriate when a whole loaf of bread is used:

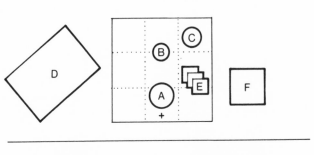

A—Paten   D—Missal Stand
B—Chalice   E—Purificators
C—Flagon or Cruet   F—Burse

If hosts are used, the following arrangement may be employed:

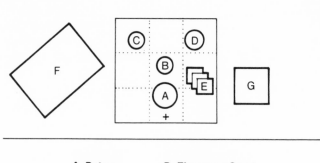

A–Paten   D–Flagon or Cruet
B–Chalice   E–Purificators
C–Ciborium or   F–Missal Stand
    Host Box   G–Burse

When additional chalices are needed for the service, they are brought to the altar and filled just before the distribution; only one chalice is on the altar for the Great Thanksgiving.

Other Preparations

Depending on local practices, the altar guild may have additional responsibilities in preparing for the Holy Communion.

In some congregations, Communion registration cards are placed in pew racks in order that a record can be kept of communicants. It is also important to be sure that sharpened pencils are in place.

In congregations where the common cup is not used, it is necessary for trays of individual glasses to be set out for distribution as communicants approach the altar. These glasses should never be prefilled, because that practice weakens the symbolism of our oneness in Christ and suggests an overly individualistic understanding of the sacrament.

When the elements are to be carried to the sick and homebound following the congregational service (using the rite of Distribution of Communion to Those in Special Circumstances, *Occasional Services*, pp. 76–81), adequate bread and wine must be provided prior to the service. In addition, the vessels for carrying the elements and the purificators need to be prepared.

Following the Service

After the liturgy is concluded, all of the eucharistic vessels and linens are removed from the chancel and taken to the sacristy for cleaning. Unused hosts are stored in a cool and dry place for future use, keeping separate those which have been consecrated. The remains of a loaf of bread should be eaten by the ministers, and shared with others if a large amount remains. Wine remaining in the chalice may be consumed by the ministers or poured into a piscina (a special drain going directly into the ground) or onto the ground.

Vessels are washed in hot soapy water and dried with soft cloths. Once cleaned, they should be handled with soft, dry gloves or cloths in order to prevent marking them. If polishing is needed, see the instructions in chapter 5 or as provided by the manufacturer.

All sacramental linens should be laundered and ironed after each use. Instructions for cleaning and stain removal are provided in chapter 5.

Eucharistic Bread Recipes

Pita

Pita is a flat, round, hollow bread (sometimes referred to as "pocket bread") which is eaten extensively in biblical lands. It is good for sacramental use because of its size, shape, and ease in handling. The following recipe is from Israel, courtesy of Avraham Har.

1. Dissolve 2 packages of yeast in 1 cup of lukewarm water.
2. Add 1 teaspoon of salt and 2½ cups of white flour to the water, and stir.
3. Knead lightly, and let the dough rise in a warm place for approximately 1 hour.
4. Knead the dough again.

5. Divide the dough into 8 equal parts. Form each part into a ball, and place on floured waxed paper.
6. Let the balls rise again for about 30 minutes.
7. Preheat the oven to 500 degrees Fahrenheit for at least 15 minutes.
8. Roll each ball on floured paper into a circle about 4 inches in diameter.
9. Flour 2 cookie sheets. Arrange 4 balls on each sheet.
10. Place the cookie sheets in the middle of the oven, and bake for about 3 minutes. The bread will look puffed in the middle, and the outside will be off-white with brown spots.

After cooling, the pita bread should be wrapped tightly to prevent drying. It may be stored in a refrigerator for several days. For longer storage, wrap well and freeze.

Flat Whole Wheat Bread

This recipe makes 4 flat 10-inch loaves, each of which will serve about 200 communicants. It is provided by Pat Frost, of St. Paul Lutheran Church, New City, New York.

1. Preheat oven to 375 degrees Fahrenheit.
2. Mix well together the following ingredients:
     6½ cups whole wheat flour
     ¼ cup olive oil
     2 tablespoons honey
     1 teaspoon salt
     2½ cups warm milk
     2 eggs
3. Divide the dough into 4 sections. Knead each section on a floured breadboard, and roll out each to make a 10-inch circle.
4. Slightly oil cookie sheets with a paper towel. On cookie sheet, carefully score each loaf vertically and horizontally, with spaces about 5/8 inch wide; do not score through to bottom.
5. Bake for 20 minutes.
6. Put on racks to cool.

These loaves may be frozen for storage. The recipe may be halved.

White Communion Bread

The following is adapted from a Coventry Cathedral recipe. It makes 4 to 6 loaves.

1 package active dry yeast

½ cup warm water (110–15 degrees Fahrenheit)

1¾ cups lukewarm milk (scalded then cooled)

7–7½ cups flour

3 tablespoons sugar

1 tablespoon salt

2 tablespoons shortening

In bowl, dissolve yeast in water. Sift flour. Add milk, sugar, salt, shortening, and half of flour to yeast and water mixture. Beat until smooth. With hand, mix in enough remaining flour until dough cleans the bowl. Turn onto lightly floured board. Cover; let rest 10–15 minutes. Knead 10 minutes until smooth. Place in greased bowl; bring greased side up. Cover with cloth. Let rise in warm place (85 degrees Fahrenheit) until double, about 1 or 2 hours.

Punch down, and turn out on floured board. Divide dough into 4 to 6 loaves (2½ ounces each). Cover, and let rest for 10 minutes. Roll out each loaf with a rolling pin into a 4-inch round. Mark with a deep cross. Arrange on a flat cookie sheet. Let rise in warm place for 40–50 minutes.

Heat oven to 425 degrees Fahrenheit. Bake 15 minutes or until golden brown. Cool slowly away from direct drafts.

8

The Word:
Place and Preparation

Our worship is centered around the Word and the Sacraments, and the worship space reflects these focuses. The font is the place of Holy Baptism, the altar is the place of the Holy Communion, and the pulpit is the primary place of the proclamation of the Word of God. The pulpit—also known as reading desk or ambo—symbolizes the preaching authority of the church.

Pulpits, as we know them, have not always been used in Christian worship. In the earliest centuries of the church, when Christians met in homes for worship, preaching was usually done from the midst of the gathered people. In the fourth century, basilicas began to be built for worship. The altars were free-standing, and the bishop preached from his chair in the apse, behind the altar; other clergy preached from the altar steps or from an ambo (similar to a lectern). In the Middle Ages, as churches became larger, pulpits began to be used. Often the pulpit was placed part of the way back in the nave (on the side), in order that the sermon could be heard by everyone. Pulpits grew large and were often decorated ornately. Another development was having two "places of the Word"—a higher pulpit or lectern for the reading of the gospel, and a less prominent lectern for the other lessons.

Today there is an increasing tendency once again to have only

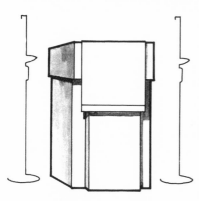

one "place of the Word," rather than a separate pulpit and lectern. This practice reflects visually the connection between the biblical readings and the sermon. Whether it is known as a pulpit, ambo, or reading desk, it should reflect the dignity and importance of the Word of God that is proclaimed from it.

A portable lectern may be brought into the worship space for those occasions when it is needed, such as Evening Prayer, the Good Friday Liturgy, and the Easter Proclamation in the Easter Vigil.

The pulpit/reading desk may have a parament known as an antependium, also called a pulpit frontal or fall. This parament should match the altar parament in color and fabric; the paraments are changed to reflect the day or season in the church year. (See chap. 7 regarding the colors.)

One way to reflect the importance of the Word of God is to flank the pulpit or reading desk with tall candlesticks. The lighted candles symbolize the light of Christ which comes to us in the Word. It is especially appropriate to place the candlesticks by the pulpit or reading desk at noneucharistic services, thus giving visual attention to the architectural center of the service.

Lectionary

The lessons should be read from a lectionary or Bible of a size and appearance that reflect the importance of the Word of God. This book may be carried in the entrance procession and placed on the pulpit or reading desk. To read the lessons from a small book or a flimsy leaflet is a poor witness to the significance of the Word.

Preparation

Prior to each service, the altar guild should be sure that the pulpit or reading desk is free of papers and books from previous services. The lectionary or Bible should be marked for the appointed readings, and placed in readiness for the entrance procession or on the pulpit/reading desk (if it is not to be carried in procession). The proper parament is placed on the pulpit or reading desk. If desired, candles are placed on the sides of the pulpit or reading desk, and the wicks are prepared for easy lighting.

For Evening Prayer or the Easter Vigil, a portable lectern is placed in readiness before the service. It may be flanked with tall candlesticks for Evening Prayer or with the paschal candlestand for the Easter Vigil.

9

Preparation for Occasional Services

In addition to liturgies that are used regularly and frequently and thus are central to the life of the congregation, such as the Holy Communion or Evening Prayer, there are various rites for specific occasions. These are known as "occasional services," and they are for use at particular times in the lives of individuals as well as in the corporate life of the church. Three of these rites (Affirmation of Baptism, Marriage, and Burial of the Dead) are provided in the *Lutheran Book of Worship*. Others of these rites are provided in a companion volume, *Occasional Services.*

Affirmation of Baptism

When the rite of Affirmation of Baptism is used for Confirmation, each confirmand kneels in front of the presiding minister in the center of the chancel. If there is no chancel rail, a prie-dieu is helpful. This is a prayer desk which assists in kneeling for the laying on of hands.

It is not necessary for confirmands to wear "robes," because they usually imply that Confirmation is a graduation. If special dress is desired, however, simple white albs are preferred, because they are reminiscent of the white baptismal garment.

Marriage

Weddings are worship services focused on God, not ceremonies focused on people. The congregation gathers to worship God who is the Source of love, and, in that worship, to witness the marriage of two persons. When this is kept in mind, many issues regarding the preparation for weddings are clarified.

Weddings are not appropriate during Holy Week, because of its solemn and penitential nature.

Paraments for weddings are in the liturgical color for the day—for whatever day or season in the church year it happens to be. It is not correct to use white paraments if white is not the appointed color in the church year. The bride and groom should be informed well in advance of the liturgical color, so that dress and flowers may be selected to coordinate with it.

The altar guild oversees the decorating of the church for weddings, and is responsible for ensuring that the altar is not obstructed and that propriety is maintained. Flowers and other decorations should not interfere with movement in the liturgy, and all decorations and floral arrangements should be appropriate for corporate worship.

Kneeling cushions or a prie-dieu are placed in the position indicated by the presiding minister. It is important that they be kept clean.

Candles near the altar are whatever would normally be there for worship. Additional candles and candelabra are optional, based on the wishes of the couple and subject to approval by the pastor. Usually the cost of any additional candles is borne by the couple. The "wedding candle" (a ceremony in which the bride and groom light a single candle and extinguish their separate candles) is theologically inappropriate and should not be used in church weddings. Bride and groom do not "extinguish" their individual lives when they are married, and to use such a ceremony reflects a deficient understanding of marriage. In addition, such a ceremony tends to overshadow the exchange of promises and the giving of rings.

The marriage service may be celebrated within the liturgy for

Holy Communion if both the bride and groom are baptized and eligible to commune according to church policy. The Eucharist is never received by the couple alone, however, because it is always a congregational celebration. If the Eucharist is celebrated, see chapter 7 regarding preparations for it.

After weddings, the altar guild is responsible for putting the chancel in order for the next worship service. If flowers are left by the wedding party, they should be used again only if they remain appropriately fresh. Otherwise, they may be taken to persons who are sick or shut-in. Empty vases should be removed from the chancel.

Burial of the Dead

Church funerals are corporate worship services, and everything about them should proclaim Christ's resurrection. Accordingly, the coffin is closed before the service begins and remains closed throughout the service.

Paraments and vestments are in the appointed color for the day or season of the church year.

Flowers may adorn the altar, and the color may be selected to coordinate with the paraments and to be appropriate to the time in the church year. Other flowers, especially large sprays with organizational or fraternal insignia, are not brought into the worship space since they tend to direct attention away from the altar. Some of these arrangements may be put in other parts of the church, such as the narthex.

Every congregation should provide a white funeral pall, which is used to cover the coffin while it is in the nave. The pall is a reminder that in Holy Baptism we have been clothed in the righteousness of Christ and that eternal life began in Baptism. The white pall thus echoes the white baptismal garment, which the fourth-century theologian John Chrysostom called the "garment of immortality." In addition, the pall en-

ables all coffins to come equally before the altar, a reminder
that God loves everyone, rich and poor alike. The pall may
be laid over the last pew in readiness for the burial liturgy. It
is placed over the coffin at the beginning of the burial liturgy,
before it is carried into the nave. The pall may be removed
from the coffin at the church door after the service in the
church.

Flowers are never placed on top of the pall. The altar guild
should ensure that the pall is clean and wrinkle-free for each
funeral in the church.

Prior to the service, the altar guild places the paschal candlestand near where the head of the coffin will be in the center
aisle. If processional torches are used instead, their stands are
placed near where the head and foot of the coffin will be. The
processional cross stand is put in its usual place in the chancel.

The coffin is carried in procession from the narthex to the
front of the nave for the burial liturgy. The order for the procession is: processional cross, paschal candle or torches, presiding
minister, assisting minister(s), pallbearers and coffin, and the
bereaved. The coffin is then placed at the front of the nave in
the center aisle at a right angle to the altar. The head of the
coffin is nearest the congregation (unless the deceased person
was ordained, in which case the head is placed closest to the
altar). The coffin is not placed parallel to the altar.

Increasingly, the burial rite is placed within the liturgy for
Holy Communion. This practice both proclaims Christ's victory over death, and gives strength to cope with grief. See chapter 7 regarding preparations for the Eucharistic liturgy.

Following the service, the pall is removed (carefully, to prevent soiling it) from the coffin at the door of the church and is
stored carefully. The processional cross and torches are stored
in the sacristy or elsewhere for future use. The paschal candle
is returned to its proper place in the chancel—near the altar
during the weeks of Easter, and near the baptismal font during
the remainder of the church year. Empty flower vases are
always removed from the chancel. Flowers not taken to the
grave may be shared with the sick and shut-in.

Service of the Word for Healing

The Service of the Word for Healing, from *Occasional Services*, is a corporate rite of readings, prayer, and the laying on of hands and anointing. It is not intended for use on Sunday mornings at the chief service of the congregation.

When this service is scheduled, the altar guild needs to prepare the oil for anointing and a purificator for wiping the minister's hands after the anointing. Both items may be placed on a credence before the service.

Oil has long been used in anointing the sick. In biblical times, oil was used as a medicine; the Good Samaritan put oil on the wounds of the wounded traveler on the road to Jericho. Oil is also a symbol of peace and of the Holy Spirit. Olive oil is traditionally used for anointing, both because it is easily absorbed by the skin and because the olive branch is an ancient symbol of life and peace.

A few drops of fragrance such as oil of bergamot or synthetic oil of cinnamon may be added to the olive oil. These fragrances are available from ecclesiastical supply stores as well as pharmacies. The oil for anointing may be placed in an oil stock. The stock contains cotton, which is moistened with the oil. Or, the fragrant oil may be stored in a cruet and then placed in a small paten or shallow bowl for the anointing.

Dedication of Worship Furnishings

This rite, from *Occasional Services*, is for dedicating or blessing new worship furnishings, such as a cross or crucifix, candles or candlesticks, sacramental vessels, paraments, funeral pall, oil, stained glass windows, chairs, and so forth. The dedication is set within the Holy Communion liturgy, just prior to the offertory prayer. When the offering (bread, wine, and money) is brought forward, the items to be dedicated may also be carried forward. A funeral pall may be placed over the chancel rail for the dedication, and then removed for the remainder of the liturgy. The altar guild cooperates with the pastor in preparing the furnishings for the dedication.

Installation of a Pastor

Occasional Services also provides this rite. An optional element in the rite is for the pastor to be presented with signs of his or her calling: a baptismal shell, a Bible, and a chalice and paten. When this is used, the items are placed on a credence before the service. After the presentation, the shell is placed on or near the font, the Bible is placed on the pulpit, and the chalice and paten are placed on the altar in preparation for the offertory.

10

Preparation for Daily Prayer Services

It is part of Old Testament as well as ancient Christian tradition to pray corporately at certain hours of the day. The principal hours for prayer are morning and evening, the times of transition between light and darkness. In our time, many congregations use Evening Prayer during Lent, and Morning Prayer is sometimes used on Sundays when the Holy Communion is not celebrated. Morning and Evening Prayer may be prayed in a simple fashion, or in an augmented form on Sundays and festivals.

The daily prayer services do not center about the altar, since they do not involve the celebration of Holy Communion. Instead, the heart of the daily prayer rites is the reading of Scripture. Accordingly, these services center on a reading desk, which may be flanked with a tall candle on each side. If the nave has flexible seating, the chairs may be arranged in facing rows, with the reading desk at one end. If seating is not flexible, the reading desk may be placed in the center of the chancel. If a portable reading desk is not available, the candles or torches may be placed at the sides of the lectern or pulpit.

The traditional vestments for daily prayer are cassock and surplice. An alb may be substituted. The stole is not worn unless there is a sermon.

For festive daily prayer services, it is traditional for the principal leader to wear a cope. The cope is an ornate cloak or cape which is open in the front, fastened near the neck with a clasp (known as a morse). The cope is worn in the appointed liturgical color for the day or season. It is worn over the surplice or alb.

Morning Prayer

Morning Prayer, also known as Matins, gives glory to God for the resurrection, symbolized by the light of the new day.

In preparation for this service, the reading desk is put in its place (see above) and a Bible is placed on it with the readings marked.

On Sundays, particularly during the weeks of Easter, the Paschal Blessing may conclude Morning Prayer. Because it is a remembrance of Baptism and a celebration of Easter, the Paschal Blessing is led from the font. Water is placed in the font before the service. At the conclusion of the Paschal Blessing, the leader may sprinkle the congregation three times with water from the font, using an evergreen bough. The sprinkling is a traditional remembrance of Baptism. When this rite is used, the altar guild needs to place an evergreen bough near the font before the service.

Evening Prayer

Also known as Vespers, Evening Prayer is a service of darkness and light, contemplation, Scripture readings, and prayer. It derives from the ancient practice of lighting lamps at sunset, and the initial emphasis in Evening Prayer is Christ as the Light of the world. This emphasis is enhanced dramatically when Evening Prayer begins with a procession in which a large lighted candle is carried into the darkened nave. This candle is as large as a paschal candle, but the paschal candle itself should not be used; the two candles have different symbolism. In preparation for the procession with light, the altar guild should place a stand for the candle in the center of the chancel or in the midst of the congregation. At festive times of the year (particularly on festivals of light such as Christmas, the Epiphany, the Transfiguration, and Easter), the congregation may be given hand candles for lighting during the singing of the *Phos hilaron*, "Joyous light of glory." Preparations need to be made by the altar guild for the distribution and collection of the hand candles.

The traditional evening Psalm is 141, and because of the text, incense is appropriate during its singing: "Let my prayer rise before you as incense." Incense is a historic symbol of prayer ascending to God. In addition, incense is a visible reminder that our sinfulness is covered with Christ's righteousness. Incense may be used in various ways. The most modest is to place some burning sticks of incense in a container which is filled with sand; the container may be placed near the stand in which the Evening Prayer candle will be set. Another practice is to light two or three pieces of charcoal in a thurible before the service; during Psalm 141, three spoonsful of incense are sprinkled on the charcoal, and one of the worship leaders then incenses the candle, the Bible, the altar, the other worship leaders, and the congregation. When this procedure is used, the altar guild places the stand for the thurible near the front of the worship space, puts the boat (the container for the incense) and spoon nearby, and prepares the thurible and charcoal. After the service, the charcoal is disposed of safely, and the thurible, stand, boat, and spoon are stored in the sacristy.

A prie-dieu may be used for the litany in Evening Prayer. It may be placed in front of the chair for the leader of the litany. Provision may be made for kneeling for the other worship leaders.

Prayer at the Close of the Day

Compline, as this service is traditionally known, is a simple and quiet rite of prayer and meditation. No special arrangements are needed for it, beyond the placement of the reading desk and its candles.

11

Preparation for the Church Year

The church year is a wonderful way in which we recall and celebrate the mighty acts of God. It is a reminder of God's constant activity—not only God's interventions into human history, but also his grace-filled activity among us now. Through the liturgical year we realize that we are a part of God's ongoing saving and loving activity.

For many centuries the church year calendar has shaped our worship: the readings, the sermons, the hymns and other music, the color of the paraments, and the appearance of worship space. Through a rich observance of the church year, each season and festival can make its fullest impact on the assembled congregation. The church is the grateful recipient and careful guardian of the liturgical year. Faithful observance of it is both a privilege and a responsibility. In its ministry of preparation, it is important for the altar guild to study the background and significance of the various liturgical seasons and festivals. Each day of the church year has its own unique character and message, determined by the appointed lessons for the day. Close attention to these lessons enables us to celebrate meaningfully the events in the life of our Lord and in church history.

The church year consists most basically of two parts. The

first half recalls and celebrates the life, death, and resurrection of Christ. This is the festival half of the year, and it in turn has two divisions. The Christmas cycle consists of the seasons of Advent, Christmas, and Epiphany. During this time the church focuses on the prophecies and events surrounding the incarnation. The Easter cycle is composed of the seasons of Lent and Easter, from Ash Wednesday through the Day of Pentecost. During these weeks we prepare for and observe the events surrounding our Lord's passion, death, and resurrection, and his sending of the Holy Spirit.

The second half of the church year is a more ordinary, nonfestival time. It is the season after Pentecost, known as the Time of the Church. This season begins with the Holy Trinity (First Sunday after Pentecost) and concludes with the festival of Christ the King (Last Sunday after Pentecost). During these weeks, the church concentrates on Christ's public ministry— his sermons, parables, and miracles. It is a time of growth in faith, hope, and love—and thus green paraments are used as a symbol of this growth.

Principal festivals of the church year are Easter Day, the Ascension of Our Lord, the Day of Pentecost, the Holy Trinity, Christmas Day, and the Epiphany of Our Lord. Interspersed throughout the year are lesser festivals, commemorations, days commemorating events in church history, and other occasions.

Advent

Advent consists of the four weeks before Christmas. The name of this first season of the liturgical year comes from a Latin word which means "coming." Advent focuses on this "coming" in three ways: Christ coming in the past as the baby at Bethlehem, Christ coming in the present in Word and Sacraments and in the fellowship of the church, and Christ coming again in the future at the end of time. In Advent we prepare for the celebration of Christ's coming in the incarnation, but more importantly we prepare for his second coming, when he will make all things new and judge the world in righteousness.

The preferred color for Advent is blue, the color of hope. The alternate color is purple, the royal color of the coming King. Blue, however, helps make apparent the differences between Advent and Lent.

One of the themes of Advent is darkness, and it is thus appropriate to use fewer candles during these four weeks. An Advent wreath may be hung or set near the altar. The wreath is a circle with four candles, and it may be covered with greens. The candles may all be white or blue, or perhaps purple if purple paraments are used. The earlier practice of using three purple candles and one pink candle no longer reflects our calendar and lectionary. On the First Sunday in Advent, the first candle is lighted during the Psalm following the First Lesson. On the Second Sunday in Advent, the first candle is lighted prior to the service, and the second candle is lighted during the Psalm. An additional candle is thus lighted during each Sunday in Advent until all four are lighted.

Advent is a time for visual restraint and simplicity. It is appropriate to omit altar flowers during these weeks of preparation, in order to provide a marked contrast with the festivity of Christmas. When there are no flowers, vases are removed from the chancel.

Advent should not be confused with Christmas. Christmas decorations, such as a Christmas tree, should not appear during Advent.

Christmas

Christmas is the festive celebration of the Nativity of our Lord, the Word made flesh. This celebration lasts for twelve days—from Christmas Eve through Epiphany Eve.

The liturgical color for Christmas is white, symbolizing the light and purity of Christ and our great joy at his birth. White is used for the twelve days of Christmas, except for the festivals of St. Stephen (December 26) and of the Holy Innocents (December 28), when red is used in observance of their martyrdom.

Greens and wreaths may be placed in the nave and narthex,

and the chancel may be adorned with abundant poinsettias. Plants, however, are never placed on the altar itself, nor should it be obstructed by decorations. If there is sufficient room, a Christmas tree (never artificial) may be set up. The tree may be bare or decorated with white lights and chrismons. If lights are used, the tree should be made fireproof. Chrismons (taken from the word "Christ monograms") are symbols of Christ which may be made by the altar guild or other members of the parish. Decorations for Christmas should not be put up until after worship on the Fourth Sunday in Advent, because early decorating robs both Advent and Christmas of their full meaning.

Especially for Christmas Eve services, candles may be placed in windows of the nave and on the ends of pews as brilliant symbols of Christ, the Light of the world. If hand candles are distributed to worshipers, all fire safety precautions should be taken. For example, the altar guild should be certain that fire extinguishers are charged and readily accessible.

A Christmas creche may be placed near the altar, although it should not detract from the prominence of the altar itself. The figures may be carried in the entrance procession on Christmas Eve or Day and then placed in the creche. The figures of the magi should be reserved until Epiphany. During the season of Christmas, the magi may be placed on a window or table near the rear of the nave or in the narthex, as a reminder of their journey to Bethlehem and of the relationship between Christmas and Epiphany.

The altar guild needs to be prepared for large numbers of communicants at Christmas liturgies and should have adequate supplies of bread and wine on the offertory table or credence, and an ample number of purificators on the credence.

Epiphany

The Epiphany of our Lord is celebrated on January 6, marking the manifestation of Christ to the whole world. The coming of the magi to Bethlehem is reported in the gospel reading for this festival; this event may be made vivid by adding the figures of the magi to the creche during the entrance procession. Figures of the shepherds and perhaps the animals may be removed in advance.

White is the appointed color for Epiphany, a reminder that it is a festival of light.

On Epiphany Eve or following the Epiphany Day liturgy, there may be a ceremony of the burning of the greens. This may take place in the church parking lot or another safe place. Municipal permission and/or fire protection may be necessary.

The Epiphany Season

The first and last Sundays after the Epiphany are festivals. The Second through the Eighth Sundays after the Epiphany use green paraments as a symbol of our growth in knowing Jesus as God's Son.

The Baptism of Our Lord

The First Sunday after the Epiphany is the Baptism of Our Lord, in observance of his Baptism by St. John the Baptist in the Jordan River and, in that event, Jesus' designation as the Son of God. Paraments for this day are white, since it is a festival of Christ. A baptismal festival may be held on this day (see chap. 6 regarding preparations for Holy Baptism).

The Transfiguration of Our Lord

The Transfiguration of Our Lord is celebrated on the Last Sunday after the Epiphany as a climax to the season and a prelude to Lent. Paraments for the Transfiguration are white.

Ash Wednesday

Since at least the seventh century, Ash Wednesday has been observed as the first day of Lent. The name is taken from the ancient tradition of placing ashes on the foreheads of penitents. In the biblical tradition, ashes represent God's condemnation of sin; human dependence on God for life; humiliation and repentance. Ashes are a reminder of death: "earth to earth, ashes to ashes, dust to dust."

Ashes for the imposition are made from palms from the

previous year's observance of the Sunday of the Passion. The palms are cut into small pieces and burned with rubbing alcohol or solid fuel firestarters. After enough has been burned, work the ash through a fine wire mesh sieve. The ash may be mixed with a small amount of oil or water and placed in a small bowl or other container for the imposition. A lavabo bowl and towel will need to be provided for cleansing the minister's hands after the imposition of ashes.

Ash Wednesday, the most penitential day of the church year, may occur between February 4 and March 10.

Paraments for Ash Wednesday may be black (the color of ashes, humiliation, and mourning) or purple (the color of penitence).

Flowers are not appropriate on Ash Wednesday, and the empty vases should also be removed from the chancel. Other festive decorations, such as banners, are also removed. From Ash Wednesday through the Saturday of Holy Week, crosses, pictures, and statues may be veiled with unbleached linen or purple fabric, as a demonstration that Lent is a time for austerity and purification.

Holy Communion is celebrated on Ash Wednesday.

Lent

Lent is the forty-day season (not including Sundays) of preparation for Easter. Traditionally, Lent has two primary themes— Baptism and penitence—both as preparation for a worthy celebration of the paschal feast. Lent does not focus on our Lord's passion; that is the focus of Holy Week.

Paraments for Lent are purple, the color of penitence.

Flowers, being a symbol of joy, may be omitted during Lent in order to help the congregation absorb the penitential character of the season. Empty vases, of course, are always removed when not in use.

The Sunday of the Passion

The first day of Holy Week is the Sunday of the Passion, also known as Palm Sunday. The mood of this day, reflecting its double name, is a mixture of triumph and tragedy. We observe both Christ's triumphant entry into Jerusalem as well as his death on the cross.

Paraments are scarlet, the dark red color of blood. The alternate color is purple, the penitential color of Lent. It is good to have scarlet, however, to help distinguish Holy Week from the remainder of Lent.

Palms may replace flowers in the chancel for this day.

The altar guild is usually responsible for obtaining and preparing a sufficient quantity of palm branches for this day's procession. Several palm branches should be saved and dried for making ashes for the following year's Ash Wednesday liturgy.

The presiding minister may wear a scarlet or purple cope during the entrance rite on the Sunday of the Passion.

Maundy Thursday

Maundy Thursday recalls the institution of the Eucharist during the Last Supper in the Upper Room. The name of the day is from the Latin word *mandatum*, which means command. It refers to Jesus' words at the Last Supper, "A new commandment I give to you, that you love one another."

Paraments for Maundy Thursday are scarlet or white. Altar flowers are appropriate and should coordinate with the color of the paraments.

Holy Communion is always celebrated on Maundy Thursday. If your parish usually uses hosts (wafers), Maundy Thursday is a day to consider using real bread in order to emphasize the meal character of this sacrament.

A foot-washing ceremony, emphasizing Jesus' servanthood, is an optional part of the Maundy Thursday liturgy. A basin, a pitcher of hot water (so that it is still warm by the time of the foot-washing), an apron, and lavabo bowl and towel for the presiding minister, and a chair and towel for each participant need to be prepared before the service.

Following the Maundy Thursday liturgy, the altar is stripped as a symbolic remembrance of Christ's humiliation by the soldiers. The altar guild may be asked to assist the presiding minister by carrying the eucharistic vessels, candles, ornaments, linens, paraments, and all other furnishings into the sacristy. The sacristy should be clean and ready for all of these items. During the stripping of the altar, a cantor or the choir sings Psalm 22 and/or 88. The chancel and altar remain bare until the Easter Vigil.

Maundy Thursday is the first day of the Triduum, the three days of intense observance of the paschal mystery. Beginning with Maundy Thursday evening, the Triduum concludes Easter Evening. It is the most sacred and important time of the entire church year.

Good Friday

The original name of this day was probably "God's Friday." It is a day to celebrate the sacrifice on the cross of Christ, our Passover Lamb. The altar is bare of all linens and other furnishings. It is preferable for paraments to be omitted on Good Friday, but if they are used, they should be scarlet or black. Flowers are not used on Good Friday.

It is not Lutheran custom to celebrate Holy Communion on Good Friday; this day's focus is the cross. The altar is not used at all during the Good Friday liturgy. Instead, the rite centers at one or more reading desks.

A large rough-hewn wooden cross may be prepared for the Good Friday Liturgy in the *Lutheran Book of Worship*. It may be placed in the narthex in readiness for its procession near the conclusion of the liturgy, or it may be placed in front of the altar (leaning against the altar or the Communion rail, or placed in a stand). A tall, lighted candle may be placed on a floor stand on each side of the cross.

If the service of Tenebrae is used, the altar guild will need to prepare a triangular candelabrum known as the Tenebrae hearse. Candles are extinguished individually following the reading of each Psalm, representing humankind falling away from Christ. The paschal candle is not used in Tenebrae; it is reserved for Easter itself.

The Vigil of Easter

The Easter Vigil is the most dramatic liturgy of the year, the climax of all of our spiritual preparations during Lent and Holy Week. It is a liturgy filled with contrasts between light and darkness, freedom and bondage, life and death. The Easter Vigil liturgy consists of four parts: the Service of Light, the Service of Readings, the Service of Holy Baptism, and the Service of Holy Communion.

Easter preparations are made with white paraments and flowers. Linens and ornaments that had been removed on Maundy Thursday are now replaced.

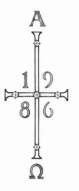

The paschal candle leads the Easter Vigil procession, and its stand should be placed in readiness near the center approach to the altar. A new paschal candle is normally acquired each year for this service. A cross, the Greek letters *alpha* and *omega*, and numerals of the current year are inscribed on the candle before the service. Traditionally the presiding minister, while doing so, says the words "Christ yesterday and today [cross]; the beginning and the end [*alpha* and *omega*]; his are all times [1] and all ages [9]; to him be glory and dominion [8], through all the ages of eternity [6]. Amen." Grains of incense are placed in readiness near the candle stand, for insertion during the Easter Proclamation.

A large fire may be built in a brazier or on the ground outside the church building, in preparation for the lighting of the paschal candle. If such a fire is not feasible, it may be struck from flint and steel.

Four to twelve biblical readings are used in the Vigil, and they should be marked in the Bible for the convenience of the lectors.

The usual preparations are made for Holy Baptism (see chap. 6). Even if Holy Baptism is not actually celebrated at the Easter

Vigil, the renewal of baptismal vows will occur, and the font should be filled with water, or a filled ewer may be placed near the font. An evergreen bough for sprinkling may be placed near the font for use during the renewal of baptismal vows.

The usual preparations are made for the Eucharist (see chap. 7). Consider using a loaf of raised bread as a symbolic reminder of our Lord's resurrection.

Easter

The festival of the Resurrection of Our Lord is the queen of all Christian festivals, and all preparations for its celebration should make its significance apparent. All of the furnishings and appointments should be thoroughly cleaned and polished. The best linens should be used, and they should be spotlessly white and newly ironed. Gold paraments may be used on Easter Day; white paraments are used during the rest of the Easter season. All paraments and vestments should be cleaned and ironed in preparation for the Easter celebration.

White or gold flowers are appropriate, and abundant Easter lilies and other flowers (including tulips, daffodils, and blooming azaleas) may be used to adorn the chancel. Flowers and plants, however, are never placed on the altar itself. All decorations should serve to direct worshipers' attention to the altar, the paschal candle, the font, and the pulpit or reading desk.

The paschal candle in its floor stand is placed near the gospel side of the altar (the left side as one faces the altar). It is lighted for all worship services from Easter Eve through the Day of Pentecost, as a reminder of the unity of these great fifty days of celebration.

The Eucharist should never be excluded from any Easter liturgy, since Easter is the paschal feast. The altar guild will need to prepare for large numbers of communicants, having adequate supplies of bread, wine, and purificators ready for use. (See chap. 7.)

Easter Day occurs between March 22 and April 25. The Easter celebration lasts for fifty days, and it is helpful to have abundant flowers throughout the season (replacing them with fresh flowers as necessary, of course).

The Ascension of Our Lord

The festival of the Ascension is forty days after Easter, and it celebrates Christ's triumphant ascension from the Mount of Olives to heaven.

White paraments are used, and white flowers are fitting.

The paschal candle may be extinguished at the reading of the gospel on Ascension Day. However, it is better to allow the candle to burn through the Day of Pentecost. Regardless of when it is extinguished, it is moved after that service to its place near the font (where it is lighted only on days when Holy Baptism is celebrated).

The Day of Pentecost

The Day of Pentecost occurs fifty days after Easter. It celebrates the time when the Holy Spirit descended to the believers gathered in Jerusalem. It is, therefore, a day when decorations and ceremonies should be reminders of the Spirit.

Bright red paraments are used on the Day of Pentecost, reminders of the fire of the Spirit. Red gladioli may be used for altar flowers, since their shape suggests tongues of fire. To emphasize the importance of this festival, the chancel may be adorned with red geraniums or other red flowers. They should be arranged to call attention to the altar, although plants and flowers are never placed on the mensa of the altar. Following Pentecost worship services, the geraniums may be planted on the church grounds.

Pentecost is an appropriate day for full and festive processions, and banners may be made in preparation for the procession. Bells may be attached to the banners to add a joyous note to the day. The presiding minister may wear a red cope for the Pentecost procession.

Holy Communion is normally celebrated on this festival, and the altar guild will make the usual preparations. (See chap. 7.)

Since the Day of Pentecost is an appropriate time for Holy Baptism as well as for Affirmation of Baptism (Confirmation), the altar guild should seek advance instructions from the pastor. (See chap. 6 regarding Baptism, and chap. 9 regarding Confirmation preparations.)

The Season after Pentecost

Except for festivals, Sundays after Pentecost use green paraments as a reminder that this is a season of spiritual growth.

The Holy Trinity

This festival occurs on the First Sunday after Pentecost, and it celebrates the doctrine of the Trinity, one God in three persons. Paraments are white.

Reformation Day

Reformation Day occurs on October 31, but it may be observed on the Sunday preceding that date. It is a day for giving thanks for Martin Luther and the other reformers, but it also calls attention to the ongoing need for renewal of the church. Paraments are bright red.

All Saints' Day

This festival commemorates all the baptized people of God who have died in the faith. All Saints' Day is November 1, but it may be observed on the Sunday following that date. The liturgical color is white.

Thanksgiving

Although it is a civil rather than a religious holiday, it has become common for churches to hold worship services on Thanksgiving Eve or Day. The liturgical color is white. Restrained decorations of the fruits of the earth—such as grapes, sheaves of grain, ears or stalks of corn—are appropriate, but should not draw attention away from the altar.

Since the word Eucharist comes from the Greek word for thanksgiving, it is fitting to celebrate Holy Communion at

Thanksgiving. Real bread rather than wafers may be used, as a reminder that God uses the fruits of the earth for God's gracious purposes.

Christ the King

The last Sunday after Pentecost celebrates the kingship of Christ and is so named. The liturgical color is white.

12

Organization

To be effective servants of the liturgy, an altar guild needs to be organized in a way that facilitates its work. Criteria for membership and principles of organization are established by the pastor and the parish worship committee, and are approved by the church council. A sample constitution is included in appendix B of this book.

Membership

An important qualification for all members of the altar guild is a sense of awe in the presence of the Holy God. This awe gives rise to the spirit of reverence that is so essential to the altar guild's work. The ministry of liturgical preparations is a high privilege for a Christian, and dedicated altar guild members will carry out their responsibilities with awe, joy, gratitude, and love for their Lord. Tasks of the altar guild are not a burden but a delight, not a duty but a high privilege. There is no room in the altar guild for complaining or grumbling. If the work cannot be done with joy and a sense of privilege, a replacement should be sought.

Another important characteristic is humility. While it is necessary for altar guild members to be skilled in various ways, each member is only one among many servants of the liturgy. The privilege of serving God is shared with other altar guild members, and with the presiding minister, assisting ministers, acolytes, ushers, and worship committee members. Large egos and prima donna attitudes do not belong in this work. Humility enables the cooperative spirit that is vital in working with the others who also serve the liturgy.

Members of the altar guild should be communicant members of the congregation, regular in worship attendance, frequent in receiving Holy Communion, always willing to learn, and eager to give priority in the use of time to the altar guild. To a great degree the worship life of the parish depends on the altar guild, and members should in turn be reliable, cooperative, and committed to their work.

With the advice of the parish worship committee, the pastor invites selected persons to membership on the altar guild. While the guild should be open to new members, it may not always be wise to issue a public invitation for volunteers, since that could result in members who are ill-equipped by attitude or skill.

Altar guild membership should not be limited to women. Men can serve the church as well as learn much about worship through service in the altar guild. Often it works well to have couples serve as working teams. Youth also have a place in this ministry of liturgical preparations. It can be a significant experience in both learning and service to have youth who are preparing for Confirmation serve as associate members in the altar guild. Youth might be invited to assist their parents who are guild members.

Since the work of the altar guild involves liturgical knowledge and many skills, it may be helpful to have new or prospective altar guild members serve six to twelve months as apprentices. Full membership may be granted after the satisfactory completion of this training period.

If there are enough skilled persons in the parish, membership may be rotating. Rotation not only involves more persons in worship preparation, but also prevents the altar guild from becoming a clique. Rotating membership, however, requires a serious and intensive ongoing training program. In any event, membership should include persons with the various skills of sewing and needlework, flower arrangement, chancel decoration, laundering and ironing of linens and vestments, polishing worship ornaments, cleaning the chancel and its furnishings, scheduling committees or work teams, keeping financial records and ordering supplies, and planning and conducting meetings.

Training

It is very important for members of the altar guild to know not only what to do, but also why. For example, it is important not only to know the proper liturgical color to be used for a given day, but also the meaning of that color and day or season. Study should be a part of every altar guild meeting. Education and training for membership should begin with the basic question, What is worship? Who is God, and why do we worship God? History and theology are involved as members learn about the development and meaning of worship space, the church year, and the liturgy. The background and meaning of worship furnishings and practices, symbolism and colors, are taught. The meaning of Holy Baptism and Holy Communion, and of the elements and vessels involved in their celebration, should be covered thoroughly and reviewed regularly. The use and meaning of other appointments and practices is also important. What does the paschal candle symbolize? When is it lighted? Why is it placed at the font after the season of Easter? Why do we strip the altar on Maundy Thursday? Why do we use a funeral pall, and why is it white? These and many other questions should be covered regularly during altar guild meetings.

Training also involves the practical skills necessary in vesting the altar, preparing for the sacraments, cleaning the chancel appointments, arranging items needed for a liturgy, changing paraments, caring for linens and vessels, preparing for the various days in the church year, preparing for weddings, funerals, and other occasional services, and carrying out other responsibilities indicated by the pastor. In all of these tasks, however, it is important that altar guild members learn about and understand the meaning as well as receive the practical instructions about how to do them.

The pastor usually does most of the training. For new members there will usually be special training sessions. For all other altar guild members, continuing education is carried out during the study periods at regular meetings of the guild. Information about these study sessions is provided in chapter 13.

Installation

As a way of recognizing the ministry of the altar guild, members may be installed during a congregational worship service. An installation rite is provided in appendix C of this book. The installation is set within the liturgy for Holy Communion, between the offertory and the offertory prayer.

The installation may be held whenever new members have been trained and are admitted to the guild. It may be useful to schedule installation once each year.

Officers

Competent and dedicated officers are essential to a well-functioning altar guild. The presiding officer (who may be called president or director) works closely with the pastor and the parish worship committee; this officer may be appointed by the pastor with the advice and approval of the worship committee and the church council, or be elected by the guild. The presiding officer conducts meetings, assigns and supervises the work of the guild, submits annual budget requests to the parish worship committee, sees that supplies are ordered, and carries out plans and directions from the pastor and parish worship committee. This officer usually also serves as a member of the parish worship committee. A written report of activities is provided by the president/director to the church council for the annual report to the congregation.

Other officers may be elected by the altar guild members at an annual organizational meeting.

A vice president or assistant director presides when the president/director is absent. This officer also assists the president/director in the coordination and supervision of the altar guild. He or she attends meetings of the parish worship committee in the absence of the president/director.

The secretary keeps a record of meetings and schedules, notifies members of meetings and assignments, and keeps an inventory of supplies and appointments.

The treasurer is responsible for the altar guild's financial transactions and records. This officer assists the president/director in preparing a proposed budget each year, and provides an annual written financial report to the church council for inclusion in the annual report to the congregation.

Committees

A simple way to organize the altar guild is into monthly committees. Each month, the members on that committee are responsible for all tasks.

Another way to organize is to divide the altar guild into several working committees, and to have one or two members of each committee serve each month. Committee memberships may rotate each year, so that all members learn several phases of the work.

While the number and organization of committees will depend on the size and worship schedule of each parish, the following schema is adaptable to most parishes. (Adapted from Ralph R. Van Loon, *Parish Worship Handbook* [Philadelphia: Parish Life Press, 1979], 44–45.)

The housekeeping committee sees that the chancel is clean for each worship service (in cooperation with the church sexton), launders and irons the fair linen monthly or as needed, changes paraments as indicated by the church year calendar, replaces candles as necessary, cleans and polishes worship appointments as needed, and sees that the altar service book and other items needed by ministers and acolytes are properly placed for each worship service. See chapter 5 for more information about these tasks.

The Communion committee vests the chalice with purificator, paten, pall, veil, and burse (containing corporal and adequate purificators), and places it on the credence prior to each service of Holy Communion. This committee also places the wine (in a flagon or cruet) and the bread (covered, to prevent drying out) on the offertory table or credence before each service. After the service, members of this committee clean and store the vessels, properly dispose of the remaining bread and wine, and launder and iron all Communion linens. See chapter 7 for details of these responsibilities.

The vestment committee launders, irons, and mends all vestments for the ministers and acolytes as needed. Albs should be ironed (and perhaps laundered) after each wearing. This committee is responsible for the dry cleaning of chasubles and stoles as necessary. See chapter 4 for more information about vestments.

The flower committee works with others in parish leadership to determine when flowers will be arriving and from whom, and to determine what is to be done with the flowers after worship. This committee arranges the flowers (or works cooperatively with the florist in assuring appropriate colors and arrangements) and has them in place at least thirty minutes before each service; removes flowers from vases after worship, cleans and dries the vases, and removes the vases to a storage place; oversees the distribution of the flowers to the sick and shut-in; and oversees flower arrangements for weddings and funerals.

The Baptism committee is informed of each scheduled Baptism or baptismal festival, determines what items are needed (baptismal candles, baptismal garments, chrism, and towels), prepares the font (if necessary, removing the font cover and rinsing the bowl), prepares warm water in the font or ewer, and places needed items (including baptismal towel, baptismal candle, baptismal garment, chrism, and perhaps a shell) near the font. Following worship, if the water does not remain in the font at all times, it is disposed of and the font is dried; vessels are removed to the sacristy. If the font has a cover, it is replaced. See chapter 6 regarding baptismal preparations.

The occasional services committee makes preparations for

weddings, funerals, confirmation, and other occasional services. See chapter 9.

If linens, paraments, and/or vestments are sewn locally, there may also be a needlework committee for this work.

Relationships

Since worship is the central function of the church, many persons and groups share responsibility for it. Cooperation, communication, and mutual respect are crucial for the worship life of the parish. The altar guild is responsible for the ministry of liturgical preparations, but it shares its servanthood with others. Good working relationships are vital.

The pastor, by virtue of his or her ordination, has primary responsibility for the ministry of worship leadership. The pastor not only presides when the family of God gathers to worship, but also helps lead others in understanding and carrying out their ministries. The pastor trains and advises the altar guild. In turn, the members of the altar guild work closely with the pastor in preparing for worship services. The pastor should always be alert to the talents and interests of parishioners in seeking new members for the altar guild.

The parish worship committee is involved in planning for worship and, in doing so, works closely with the pastor. This committee oversees the work of the altar guild, and the president or director of the guild usually serves on this committee. When the committee's worship plans are approved by the church council, the altar guild is responsible for seeing that the necessary preparations are made. The altar guild's annual budget request is submitted to the worship committee.

All parish policies and practices are determined by the church council in cooperation with the pastor, and consistent with theology and policies of the national church body. The altar guild has input into this process through its representation on the parish worship committee. Communications with the church council are normally made through the parish worship committee.

Acolytes have an important role in parish worship. The official relationship between the altar guild and the acolytes will depend on the parish, but guild members should always stand ready to help and support acolytes. In most parishes, the altar guild is responsible for acolytes' vestments, and sometimes acolytes use the working sacristy for vesting and pre-service preparations. Members of the altar guild will want to be sure that they set an appropriate example for acolytes in their attitudes, words, and actions.

The altar guild also needs a cooperative relationship with the church sexton. The pastor and church council, with the advice of the worship committee, determine the division of responsibilities between the sexton and the altar guild. Usually the sexton cleans the chancel floor and leaves other cleaning in the chancel to the altar guild.

13

Meetings

It is helpful for the altar guild to meet monthly. These regular meetings foster good communication, provide the opportunity for continual learning, enable scheduling to occur and assignments to be made, provide for checks on members' accountability, and are a time for fellowship.

Agenda

Meetings are called to order by the president or director. The agenda is usually set forth in the local altar guild constitution, but normally it includes the following items:

Call to order
Attendance
Devotions
Study
Officers' reports
Committee reports
Old business
New business
Prayer

As a part of new business, the president/director reviews the worship schedule for the coming month(s) and makes assignments.

Refreshments may follow the business meeting.

Devotions

Devotions are an important part of this meeting. Members may take turns leading the group in devotions, and the pastor may suggest various rites to use. Possibilities from the *Lutheran Book of Worship* include Responsive Prayer 1 (p. 161) or a simplified form of Morning Prayer (p. 131) for morning meetings; Responsive Prayer 2 (p. 164) for afternoon meetings; and Responsive Prayer 2 or a simplified form of Evening Prayer (p. 142) for evening meetings. The Litany (p. 168) could be used at any time; it is especially appropriate for Lent.

For closing devotions at evening meetings, immediately before members go home, Prayer at the Close of the Day (p. 154), also known as Compline, may be used. Because this brief office is the "going to bed prayer of the church," it should come at the end of meetings, following refreshments and fellowship.

If the meeting is held on a festival or commemoration of the church year, Scripture and prayers should be selected accordingly. It is helpful to refer to the calendar (pp. 10–12) and propers (pp. 13–41) in the *Lutheran Book of Worship.*

For other days, Scripture readings may be selected from the *Lutheran Book of Worship* Daily Lectionary (p. 179). Year One lessons are read beginning in Advent preceding odd-numbered years. Year Two lessons are read beginning in Advent preceding even-numbered years.

The following prayers, from the *Lutheran Book of Worship* and *Occasional Services*, may be used for altar guild meetings:

Almighty God, we give you thanks that you provide for the work of your church through the different gifts of the members of this altar guild. Help us to recognize and act upon every opportunity for service. Guide our diversity by your one Spirit, that everything we think, say, and do may be for the common good of your church; through your Son, Jesus Christ our Lord. Amen

God of majesty, whom saints and angels delight to worship in heaven: Be with your servants who make art and music for your people, that with joy we on earth may glimpse your beauty; and bring us to the fulfillment of that hope of perfection which will be ours as we stand before your unveiled glory. We pray in the name of Jesus Christ our Lord. Amen

Lord God of our salvation, it is your will that all people might come to you through your Son Jesus Christ. Inspire our witness to him, that all may know the power of his forgiveness and the hope of his resurrection. We pray in his name. Amen

Almighty God, by our baptism into the death and resurrection of your Son Jesus Christ, you turn us from the old life of sin. Grant that we who are reborn to new life in him may live in righteousness and holiness all our days, through your Son, Jesus Christ our Lord. Amen

Almighty God, draw our hearts to you, guide our minds, fill our imaginations, control our wills, so that we may be wholly yours. Use us as you will, always to your glory and the welfare of your people; through our Lord and Savior Jesus Christ. Amen

Direct us, O Lord, in all our doings with your most gracious favor and further us with your continual help, that in all our works, begun, continued, and ended in you, we may glorify your holy name and finally, by your mercy, obtain everlasting life; through Jesus Christ our Lord. Amen

Topics for Study

The competence of the altar guild depends on good study sessions at the meetings. Included may be demonstrations of specific tasks; slides or films on symbols, architecture, the sacraments, liturgy, and the church year; and programs presented by the pastor, members, or guests. The list of possible topics is almost endless and includes the following:

Contents of the *Lutheran Book of Worship* (including the *LBW Ministers Edition*)

Contents of *Occasional Services*

Meaning of Holy Communion

Meaning of Holy Baptism

Meaning of Morning Prayer

Meaning of Evening Prayer

Meaning of Prayer at the Close of the Day

Church architecture and its symbolism
Development and structure of the church year
Meaning and customs of seasons and festivals
Meaning of parts of the liturgy
Meaning of the burial liturgy
Meaning of the marriage liturgy
Old Testament worship
New Testament worship
Worship in the early church
Luther and worship
Development and meaning of vestments
Meaning of liturgical colors
Worship furnishings and appointments
Symbols
Meaning and use of candles in worship
Eucharistic vessels and elements
Church art
Music in worship
Hymns
Psalms
Meaning of the sign of the cross
Meaning of the exchange of Peace
Rubrics

The "For Further Help" section at the end of this book includes resources that will be useful in preparing study programs. If your parish library does not include these books, it would be a worthy project for the altar guild to purchase them as gifts for the library. The pastor will also have suggestions and resources for study sessions.

Other possibilities for learning include visits to other churches to observe their worship space, furnishings, sacristies, paraments, and vestments. The synodical or district worship committee can suggest good places to visit. In addition, the parish worship committee chairperson or parish musicians may be invited to altar guild meetings to discuss their work in planning and preparing for worship. A local florist could come to discuss the care and arrangement of flowers. An architect or ecclesiastical artist might discuss the role of art and architecture in worship.

Projects

Members of the altar guild might undertake special projects from time to time, including some of the following:

1. Make banners for processions on festivals of the church year.
2. Accompany the pastor on Communion visits to shut-ins. If parish practice involves lay members taking the Communion to the sick and shut-in after Sunday morning worship, altar guild members could be involved in this ministry.
3. Exhibit and discuss linens, paraments, vessels, and vestments at catechetics classes, adult classes, worship committee meetings, church council meetings, and circle meetings.
4. Discuss with the pastor the possibility of assisting with First Communion classes.
5. Hold displays or exhibits of vessels, vestments, linens, paraments, and appointments in the narthex as a means of worship education for the parish.
6. Prepare articles for the parish newsletter on symbols and colors of the church year, or on the names and use of sacramental vessels.
7. If the parish owns historic eucharistic vessels, they might be displayed as a part of an anniversary celebration.
8. Members skilled in needlework could make wedding cushions, new paraments, new vestments, or new linens.
9. Make a set of chrismons for decorating the church Christmas tree; after they are made, a program on symbolism could be presented using the chrismons to illustrate the symbols.
10. A calendar of liturgical festivals and commemorations, with suggested Scripture readings and the appointed

colors, could be procured or prepared for distribution or sale to the congregation. If sold, proceeds could be used for books for the parish library or for new items needed by the congregation, such as a processional cross, processional torches, paschal candle and stand, white funeral pall, chasubles, copes, other new vestments, new linens, or new paraments.

11. Make bread and/or wine for sacramental use.
12. Offer to help church school teachers when lessons deal with worship, symbols, and the church year.
13. If a mission congregation is established in the region, offer assistance in organizing and training an altar guild in the new congregation.

Appendix A
Outlines of the Church Year
and Colors

Seasons and Principal Festivals

The Christmas Cycle

Advent Season—Four Sundays in Advent (blue or purple)

Christmas Season

    The Nativity of Our Lord—Christmas Eve and Christmas Day (white)

    First and Second Sundays after Christmas (white)

Epiphany Season

    The Epiphany of Our Lord (white)

    The Baptism of Our Lord—First Sunday after the Epiphany (white)

    Second through Eighth Sundays after the Epiphany (green)

    The Transfiguration of Our Lord—Last Sunday after the Epiphany (white)

The Easter Cycle

Lenten Season

    Ash Wednesday (black or purple)

    First through Fifth Sundays in Lent (purple)

Holy Week

    Sunday of the Passion—Palm Sunday (scarlet or purple)

    Monday through Wednesday (scarlet or purple)

    Maundy Thursday (scarlet or white)

Good Friday (no paraments)

Easter Season

  Vigil of Easter (white)

  The Resurrection of Our Lord—Easter Day (white or gold)

  Second through Seventh Sundays of Easter (white)

  The Ascension of Our Lord (white)

  The Day of Pentecost (red)

The Time of the Church

The Season after Pentecost

  The Holy Trinity—First Sunday after Pentecost (white)

  Second through Twenty-seventh Sundays after Pentecost (green)

  Christ the King—Last Sunday after Pentecost (white)

Lesser Festivals

Lesser festivals may have precedence over Sundays for which the color is green, and over the First and Second Sundays after Christmas.

November 30—St. Andrew, Apostle (red)

  First apostle to follow Jesus. Martyred at Patras in Greece on this date in A.D. 60.

December 21—St. Thomas, Apostle (red)

  One of the twelve apostles; was unwilling to believe in the resurrection until he had touched Jesus.

December 26—St. Stephen, Deacon and Martyr (red)

  One of the seven deacons ordained by the apostles. Was the first to die for his faith; martyred by stoning.

December 27—St. John, Apostle and Evangelist (white)

  With James and Peter, St. John was in the inner circle of the apostles. Was the only one of the apostles not to be martyred.

December 28—The Holy Innocents, Martyrs (red)

  The innocent young children of Bethlehem killed by King Herod in his attempt to destroy the infant Jesus.

January 1—The Name of Jesus (white)

  Recalls the circumcision and naming of Jesus.

January 18—The Confession of St. Peter (white)

Celebrates St. Peter's confession that Jesus is "the Christ, the Son of the living God."

January 25—The Conversion of St. Paul (white)
Celebrates the conversion of Saul the Pharisee to Paul the Christian.

February 2—The Presentation of Our Lord (white)
Recalls the presentation of Jesus in the temple by his parents, and celebrates the occasion of the *Nunc Dimittis*, the Song of Simeon.

February 24—St. Matthias, Apostle (red)
St. Matthias was selected to fill the vacancy in the twelve apostles left by Judas Iscariot's death.

March 25—The Annunciation of Our Lord (white)
Observes the angel's announcement to Mary that she would give birth to Jesus.

April 25—St. Mark, Evangelist (red)
Companion of St. Peter; author of Second Gospel. Martyred in Alexandria in A.D. 64.

May 1—St. Philip and St. James, Apostles (red)
Two apostles. The remains of both were placed in the Church of the Apostles in Rome on this date in A.D. 561.

May 31—The Visitation (white)
Marks Mary's visit to Elizabeth, and celebrates the occasion of the *Magnificat*, the Song of Mary.

June 11—St. Barnabas, Apostle (red)
Early Christian disciple who worked with St. Paul; believed to have been martyred in Cyprus in A.D. 61.

June 24—The Nativity of St. John the Baptist (white)
Celebrates the birthday of St. John the Baptist.

June 29—St. Peter and St. Paul, Apostles (red)
Celebrates the apostles' ministry to both the Jewish and gentile worlds. Both are believed to have been martyred in Rome.

July 22—St. Mary Magdalene (white)
Principal witness of the resurrection.

July 25—St. James the Elder, Apostle (red)
Brother of St. John; the only apostle whose martyrdom is recorded in Scripture (Acts 12:2)

August 15—Mary, Mother of Our Lord (white)
Honors the mother of Jesus. Celebrated on the traditional date of Mary's death.

August 24—St. Bartholomew, Apostle (red)
One of the twelve apostles; traditionally believed to have been skinned alive.

September 14—Holy Cross Day (red)
Dates from the dedication in A.D. 335 of a basilica in Jerusalem, built by Constantine, on the site of the crucifixion and resurrection.

September 21—St. Matthew, Apostle and Evangelist (red)
Roman tax collector who became a disciple. Believed to have been martyred.

September 29—St. Michael and All Angels (white)
Honors the archangel Michael. Only festival of the angels retained by Luther; also known as Michaelmas.

October 18—St. Luke, Evangelist (red)
A gentile physician, follower of Christ, and companion of St. Paul; author of the Third Gospel and Acts.

October 28—St. Simon and St. Jude, Apostles (red)
Two apostles; martyred together in Persia.

October 31—Reformation Day (red)
Anniversary of Luther's posting of his Ninety-five Theses in Wittenberg, Germany, in 1517.

November 1—All Saints' Day (white)
Commemorates all the baptized people of God who have died in the faith.

Appendix B
Constitution

A written constitution is helpful for any organization. The altar guild constitution should be written with the help of the pastor, and it is subject to approval by the parish worship committee and the church council. The following is only a sample; it needs adaptation for actual usage, to reflect local organization.

Article 1—Name

The name of this organization is the Altar Guild of (*name of congregation*).

Article 2—Purpose

1. To care for the worship space, its furnishings, linens, paraments, and appointments.
2. To prepare the worship space for all services, including Sunday worship, special services, weddings, and funerals.
3. To care for vestments of the pastor, assisting ministers, and acolytes.
4. To study and constantly grow in understanding of the worship practices of the church.

Article 3—Membership

1. The membership shall consist of a minimum of (*number*) communicant members of the parish, appointed by the pastor.

2. Membership is open to both men and women.
3. Youth may serve as associate members.

Article 4—Officers

1. The officers are: president, vice president, secretary, and treasurer.
2. The president is appointed annually by the pastor, with the advice of the parish worship committee and the approval of the church council [or: is elected annually by the guild].
3. Other officers are elected by the guild for one-year terms.
4. The officers have the following duties:
   a. The president presides at meetings; assigns and supervises the work of the guild; serves as a member of the parish worship committee; sees that plans and directions from the pastor, worship committee, and church council are carried out by the guild; and orders supplies as needed. The president and the treasurer prepare the proposed budget each year, and the president submits it to the parish worship committee. The president prepares a written report each year for the annual meeting of the congregation.
   b. The vice president presides at meetings in the absence of the president and assists the president as requested.
   c. The secretary keeps a record of meetings and schedules, notifies members of guild meetings, and keeps an inventory of supplies and worship appointments.
   d. The treasurer keeps financial records and provides a written financial report each year for the annual meeting of the congregation. The treasurer assists the president annually in the preparation of the proposed budget.

Article 5—Committees

1. The standing committees are: housekeeping, Communion, vestment, flower, Baptism, occasional services, and needlework.
2. The housekeeping committee sees that the chancel is clean and prepared for all services, cares for the fair linen and para-

ments, replaces candles, cleans and polishes worship appointments, and puts in place books and other needed items for services.

3. The Communion committee prepares the altar for each celebration of the Holy Communion, and cares for the elements, vessels, and linens.

4. The vestment committee cares for all vestments for ministers and acolytes.

5. The flower committee prepares and places all flowers in the chancel, cares for vases, and oversees the distribution of flowers to the sick and shut-in.

6. The Baptism committee prepares the font and necessary items for each Baptism.

7. The occasional services committee prepares for weddings, funerals, confirmation, and other occasional services.

8. The needlework committee oversees the making of paraments, vestments, linens, and other needlework items.

Article 6—Meetings

1. The regular monthly meetings are on:

2. The January meeting is considered the annual meeting, during which the vice president, secretary, and treasurer are elected.

3. Special meetings may be called by the president or the pastor.

4. The order of business at regular meetings is: call to order, attendance, devotions, study, officers' reports, committee reports, old business, new business, and closing prayer.

Article 7—Amendments

Amendments to this constitution may be made by a two-thirds vote of the altar guild members, and must be ratified by the church council upon recommendation by the parish worship committee.

Appendix C
Order for Installing
Altar Guild Members

This order, from *Occasional Services* (p. 143), follows the Offering and the Offertory in the Holy Communion liturgy.

Sit

The presiding minister addresses the congregation:

Dear Christian friends: Baptized into the priesthood of Christ, we all are called to offer ourselves to the Lord of the church in thanksgiving for what he has done and continues to do for us. It is our privilege to recognize and support those who are engaged in the work of this congregation, especially those in the ministry of the altar guild.

As a representative of the congregation reads a brief description of the ministry of the altar guild, the persons engaged in that ministry stand.

The presiding minister addresses those who are beginning their ministry in the altar guild:

Having offered yourselves in the altar guild ministry of this congregation, will you follow our Lord's example of humble service?

The persons being installed in the altar guild respond:
Yes, with God's help.

Stand

The presiding minister says:
Let us pray.
God of majesty, whom saints delight to worship in heaven and on earth: Bless the ministry of those serving in the altar guild, that we may know the joy of your presence and may worship to the glory of your holy name; through Jesus Christ our Lord.

The congregation responds:
Amen

The presiding minister concludes:
For all who offer themselves in your name, we give thanks, O God. Give them the joy of service, and constant care and guidance. Help us all to be both willing servants and thankful recipients of ministry, that your name be glorified, your people live in peace, and your will be done; through Jesus Christ our Lord.

The congregation responds:
Amen

The service continues with the Offertory Prayer.

Glossary

Acolyte From the Greek for "to follow"; a liturgical assistant who serves in various roles as crucifer, torchbearer, bannerbearer, bookbearer, candlelighter, and server.

Advent From the Latin for "coming"; the four weeks before Christmas which constitute the first season of the liturgical year. The color is blue or purple.

Advent Wreath A wreath with four candles, used during the four weeks of Advent.

Affirmation of Baptism Rite used for confirmation, reception of new members, and restoration to membership.

Alb Full-length white vestment used in worship since the sixth century. Usually worn with cincture.

Alms Basin Large plate in which the smaller offering plates are received.

Altar Table in the chancel used for the celebration of the Holy Communion. It is the central furnishing and focus of the worship space.

Altar Antependium Parament hung in the center of the altar, covering part of the front of the altar.

Altar Rail Railing enclosing the chancel at which people stand or kneel to receive Holy Communion.

Ambo Another name for the pulpit, reading desk, or lectern.

Amice White linen cloth resembling a collar which is often worn with an alb.

Ante-Communion That portion of the Holy Communion liturgy preceding the Great Thanksgiving.

Antependium Parament for pulpit and lectern.

Apse The semicircular (or polygonal) projection or alcove at the end of the chancel.

Ascension Principal festival occurring forty days after Easter, which celebrates Christ's ascension to heaven. The color is white.

Ashes Symbol of repentance and mortality used in the Ash Wednesday liturgy; made by burning palms from previous year's Sunday of the Passion procession.

Ash Wednesday First day of Lent;

occurs between February 4 and March 10. Name derives from the ancient practice of placing ashes on worshipers' foreheads. The color is black or purple.

Asperges Ceremony during the renewal of baptismal vows during the Easter Vigil, in which water from the font is sprinkled over the congregation as a remembrance of their Baptism.

Assisting Minister Lay or ordained person who assists the presiding minister in worship leadership.

Banner Fabric hanging carried in processions.

Baptism The sacrament of water and the Holy Spirit, in which we are joined to Christ's death and resurrection and initiated into the church.

Baptistery The place where the baptismal font is located.

Black Liturgical color for Ash Wednesday; symbolizes ashes, repentance, and humiliation.

Blue Liturgical color for Advent; symbolizes hope.

Burse Square fabric-covered case in which the Communion linens are carried to and from the altar.

Candle Tall wax light burned during worship services; symbolic of Christ, the Light of the world.

Candlelighter Device used to light and extinguish candles.

Candlestick Ornamental base holder for candle.

Cassock Full-length black vestment worn under surplice, cotta, or alb.

Censer Vessel in which incense is burned; also called thurible.

Cerecloth First cloth placed on the mensa; usually made of wax-treated linen.

Chalice Cup used for the wine in the Holy Communion.

Chancel Elevated area in front of the nave where altar and pulpit are located.

Chasuble The principal vestment for the Holy Communion liturgy; worn like a poncho by the presiding minister over alb and stole.

Choir In traditional church architecture, the part of the chancel between the nave and the sanctuary.

Chrism Fragrant oil used for anointing in Holy Baptism.

Chrismon From the words "Christ monograms"; symbols of Christ used to decorate Christmas trees.

Chrisom White garment placed on a person after Baptism as a symbol of being clothed in the righteousness and eternal life of Christ.

Christ the King The last Sunday of the church year, which celebrates the kingship of Christ. The color is white.

Christmas Principal festival of the church year which celebrates Christ's birth or nativity; also known as the Nativity of Our Lord. The color is white.

Ciborium Tall covered vessel which holds wafers for the Holy Communion.

Cincture Rope belt worn with an alb.

Compline From the Latin for "complete," referring to the prayers which completed the day's worship. An order for night prayer used as the last worship service before bed. Also known as Prayer at the Close of the Day.

Confirmation Liturgical form of Affirmation of Baptism, marking the completion of a period of instruction in the Christian faith.

Cope Long cape worn by worship leader, lay or ordained, for certain processions and ceremonial occasions.

Corporal Square white linen cloth placed on the center of the mensa, on which the eucharistic vessels are placed for the celebration of the Holy Communion.

Corpus Carved figure of Christ attached to a cross; together, cross and corpus are a crucifix.

Cotta Short white vestment worn over cassock by acolytes and choir members.

Credence Shelf or table at chancel wall which holds sacramental vessels and offering plates.

Crosier Crook-shaped staff carried by a bishop.

Crucifer The person who carries the processional cross.

Crucifix Cross with a corpus attached.

Cruet Glass vessel containing wine for the Holy Communion. An additional cruet may hold water for the lavabo.

Daily Prayer The daily services of readings and prayer, including Morning Prayer, Evening Prayer, and Prayer at the Close of the Day (Compline).

Dalmatic Eucharistic vestment sometimes worn by an assisting minister during festive celebrations of the Holy Communion.

Dossal Fabric hanging behind and above altar.

East Wall The wall behind the altar, regardless of whether the wall is geographically to the east.

Eastwall Altar An altar attached to the wall.

Easter Principal festival of the church year which celebrates Christ's resurrection. Easter Day (which occurs between March 22 and April 25) is known as the Resurrection of Our Lord, and the color is gold or white. The Easter season lasts for fifty days, and the color is white.

Easter Vigil Liturgy on Easter Eve which includes the lighting of the new fire and procession of the paschal candle, readings from Scripture, Holy Baptism and the renewal of baptismal vows, and Holy Communion. The color is gold or white.

Elements The earthly elements used in the celebration of the sacraments: bread and wine in Holy Communion, and water in Holy Baptism.

Epiphany Principal festival celebrated on January 6, marking the visit of the magi to Jesus and the consequent revelation of Christ to the whole world. The color is white.

Epistle Side The right side of the altar as the congregation faces it.

Eucharist From the Greek for "thanksgiving"; a name for the Holy Communion.

Evening Prayer An evening worship service of Scripture readings and prayer; also known as Vespers.

Ewer A pitcher used for carrying water to the baptismal font.

Fair Linen Top white linen cloth covering the mensa of the altar; symbolizing the winding sheet used in the burial of Christ's body.

Fall Term sometimes used for paraments on altar, pulpit, and lectern.

Flagon Pitcherlike vessel from which wine is poured into the chalice for the Holy Communion.

Font From the Latin for "fountain"; the pool or basin which holds water for Holy Baptism.

Fraction Ceremonial breaking of the bread in the Holy Communion liturgy.

Free-standing Altar An altar which is not attached to the wall, and behind which the ministers stand (facing the congregation) for the celebration of Holy Communion.

Frontal Parament which covers the entire front of the altar, from the top edge of the mensa down to the predella.

Frontlet Narrow altar parament usually hung in pairs and extending only part way to the predella.

Funeral Pall Large white cloth cover placed on the coffin when brought into the nave for the burial liturgy.

Gold Liturgical color for Easter Eve and Easter Day, giving special prominence to this most important festival of the year.

Good Friday The Friday in Holy Week which observes Christ's crucifixion and death. The chan-cel and altar are bare of all appointments, paraments, and linens.

Gospel Side Left side of the altar as the congregation faces it.

Gradine From the Latin for "step"; a step or shelf at the rear of the mensa of an eastwall altar, on which cross, candlesticks, and flowers are placed. Also known as retable.

Green Liturgical color for the nonfestival seasons after Pentecost and Epiphany; symbolic of growth.

Hearse A triangular candelabrum used for Tenebrae.

Holy Trinity First Sunday after Pentecost, which celebrates the doctrine of the Trinity (one God in three persons: Father, Son, and Holy Spirit). The color is white.

Holy Week The week between the Sunday of the Passion (Palm Sunday) and Easter, which recalls the events of the last days of Christ's life. The color is scarlet or purple for Sunday through Wednesday, and scarlet or white on Maundy Thursday. No paraments are used on Good Friday.

Host Wafer, made of unleavened bread, for the Holy Communion.

Host Box Short, round, covered container which holds additional hosts for the Holy Communion. Also known as pyx.

Incense Mixture of resins for ceremonial burning, symbolic of our prayers rising to God (see Psalm 141); one of the gifts of the magi to Jesus on the Epiphany.

Intinction From the Latin for "to dip"; the practice of administering the eucharistic elements by dipping the bread or host into the wine.

Laudian Frontal A type of frontal which entirely covers all sides of a free-standing altar.

Lavabo Bowl used for the act of cleansing the presiding minister's hands in the Holy Communion or after the imposition of ashes.

Lectern Reading stand in the chancel from which the Scripture lessons are read.

Lectionary The appointed system of Scripture lessons for the days of the church year. Also refers to the book that contains these readings.

Lector The assisting minister who reads the Scripture lessons.

Lent From the Anglo-Saxon for "spring"; the penitential forty-day season (excluding Sundays) before Easter, beginning with Ash Wednesday. Symbolic of Christ's forty days in the wilderness. Lent is traditionally the season when candidates prepare for Holy Baptism, which is celebrated at the Easter Vigil. The color is purple.

Lenten Veil Cloth used to cover crosses, pictures, and other objects during Lent.

Linens Refers to three groups of white linen cloths: altar linens (cerecloth, protector linen, and fair linen), Communion linens (corporal, pall, purificators, and veil), and other linens (credence linen, offertory table linen, lavabo towel, and baptismal towel).

Liturgy From the Greek for "the people's work"; the prescribed worship service of the church.

Lucernarium From the Latin for "light"; the service of light at the beginning of Evening Prayer.

Matins From the Latin for "morning"; morning service of Scripture reading and prayer; also known as Morning Prayer.

Maundy Thursday From the Latin for "commandment"; the Thursday in Holy Week which commemorates the institution of the Holy Communion. The color is scarlet or white.

Mensa From the Latin for "table"; the top of the altar.

Missal Altar service book.

Missal Stand Stand or cushion on the altar on which the altar service book is placed during the Holy Communion liturgy.

Morning Prayer Morning service of Scripture reading and prayer; also known as Matins.

Morse The clasp used to fasten a cope.

Narthex Entrance hall of a church building which leads to the nave.

Nave From the Latin for "ship"; the section of the church building between the narthex and the chancel, where the congregation gathers for worship.

New Fire The fire kindled on Easter Eve, used to light the paschal candle for the Easter Vigil. Symbolic of Christ's resurrected presence.

Occasional Service Liturgical rite used from time to time, including rites for confirmation, burial, marriage, healing, ordination, dedication of a church building, installation of a pastor, etc.

Offertory Table A small table near the rear of the nave which holds the bread and wine prior to the offertory.

Ordinary Those parts of the liturgy which do not change from week to week.

Orphrey Ornamental band on a chasuble or parament.

Pall Linen-covered square placed over rim of the chalice. (See also funeral pall.)

Palm Sunday See Sunday of the Passion.

Paraments Cloth hangings of various liturgical colors used to adorn the altar, pulpit, and lectern.

Paschal Candle Large white candle carried in procession during the Easter Vigil, and placed near the altar and lighted during the Easter season, symbolizing Christ's resurrected presence. At other times of the year, it is placed near the font and lighted for Holy Baptism, and placed at the head of the coffin for the burial liturgy.

Paten Plate used to hold bread during the Holy Communion liturgy.

Pectoral Cross A cross on a chain, worn around the neck by a bishop.

Pentecost From the Greek for "fiftieth day"; principal festival of the church year, occurring fifty days after Easter. Celebrates the descent of the Holy Spirit to the crowd gathered in Jerusalem. The color for this festival is red.

Phos Hilaron Greek name for the canticle in Evening Prayer which begins "Joyous light of glory."

Piscina A special drain in the sacristy which goes directly into the ground, used for disposal of baptismal water and wine remaining after the Holy Communion.

Prayer at the Close of the Day Night prayer service used as the last worship before retiring for the night. Also known as Compline.

Predella Raised platform in the chancel on which the altar is placed.

Presiding Minister The ordained pastor who presides at a worship service.

Prie-dieu French term for "prayer desk"; used for Daily Prayer services, confirmation, and weddings.

Processional Cross A cross or crucifix on a tall staff used to lead processions.

Processional Torch See torch.

Propers The varying portions of the liturgy which are appointed for each day of the church year; include the Prayer of the Day, Psalm, lessons, proper verse, proper offertory, and proper preface.

Protector Linen White linen cloth placed on the mensa between the cerecloth and the fair linen, to which the parament may be attached.

Pulpit Raised reading desk in the chancel from which the gospel is read and the sermon preached.

Purificator Square linen napkin used to cleanse the rim of the chalice during the distribution of Holy Communion.

Purple Liturgical color for Lent,

symbolizing penitence. Also the alternate color for Advent, symbolizing the royal color of the coming King.

Pyx See host box.

Red Bright red liturgical color, symbolic of the fire of the Holy Spirit. Used on the Day of Pentecost, Reformation Day, martyrs' days, and certain church occasions such as ordination and the dedication of a church building.

Reredos Carved stone or wood panel behind and above an altar.

Responsive Prayer Brief liturgical order of versicles and responses.

Retable A step or shelf at the rear of the mensa of an eastwall altar, on which cross, candlesticks, and flowers are placed. Also known as gradine.

Rite The text and ceremonies of a liturgical worship service.

Rubric From the Latin for "red"; a direction for the proper conduct of a worship service. Rubrics are usually printed in red.

Sacrament A rite commanded by Christ which uses an earthly element as a sign of God's grace. The two sacraments are Holy Baptism and Holy Communion.

Sacristy A room used for storage and preparation of items needed in worship; also used for vesting before services.

Sanctuary The section of the chancel which immediately surrounds the altar.

Sanctuary Lamp A constantly burning candle suspended from the ceiling or mounted on the chancel wall; in Roman Catholic and some Episcopal churches,

symbolizes the Reserved Sacrament.

Scarlet The deep red liturgical color used from the Sunday of the Passion (Palm Sunday) through Maundy Thursday. Symbolic of the blood of the Passion.

Sedilia Seats in the chancel for the worship leaders.

Sign of the Cross Gesture of tracing the outline of the cross with the hand, as a mark of belonging to Christ in Holy Baptism.

Spoon Perforated utensil used to remove foreign particles from wine in the chalice.

Stole Cloth band in liturgical color worn over the alb or surplice around a pastor's neck and hanging to the knees. Signifies ordination and the yoke of obedience to Christ.

Stripping of the Altar Ceremony at the conclusion of the Maundy Thursday liturgy, in which all appointments, linens, and paraments are removed from the altar and chancel in preparation for Good Friday. Symbolic of Christ's humiliation by the soldiers.

Sunday of the Passion The first day of Holy Week, also known as Palm Sunday. Commemorates both Christ's triumphant entry into Jerusalem and his crucifixion. The color is scarlet or purple.

Superfrontal Short parament which hangs over the front of the mensa.

Surplice White vestment worn over the cassock; used especially for Daily Prayer services.

Tenebrae From the Latin for "darkness"; a service sometimes used evenings during Holy Week, in which candles on a hearse are gradually extinguished.

Thurible Vessel in which incense is burned; also known as a censer.

Thurifer The person who carries the thurible.

Torch Large candle on a tall staff carried in processions.

Torchbearer The person who carries the processional torch.

Transfiguration Festival celebrated on the Last Sunday after the Epiphany, recalling Christ's transfiguration on the mountain. The color is white.

Triduum The Latin for "three days"; the three sacred days from Maundy Thursday evening through Easter Evening, which together celebrate the unity of the paschal mystery of Christ's death and resurrection.

Tunicle Eucharistic vestment less ornate than a dalmatic; may be worn by the junior assisting minister at festive Holy Communion services.

Veil Cloth placed over sacramental vessels before and after the celebration of Holy Communion.

Vespers From the Latin for "evening"; an evening worship service of Scripture readings and prayer. Also known as Evening Prayer.

Vigil A liturgical service on the eve of a festival, such as the Easter Vigil.

White Liturgical color used on festivals of Christ, the weeks of Christmas and Easter, The Holy Trinity, and certain saints' days. Symbolizes joy, gladness, purity, and the light of Christ.

For Further Help

Adam, Adolf. *The Liturgical Year*. New York: Pueblo Pub. Co., 1981. A helpful guide to the history and meaning of the festivals and seasons of the church year.

Bradner, John. *Symbols of Church Seasons and Days*. Wilton, Conn.: Morehouse-Barlow Co., 1977. An illustrated guide to symbols for the church year; includes helpful explanations.

Brand, Eugene L., and S. Anita Stauffer. *By Water and the Spirit*. Philadelphia: Parish Life Press, 1979. An illustrated commentary on the liturgy for Holy Baptism in the *Lutheran Book of Worship*.

Clowney, Paul, and Tessa Clowney. *Exploring Churches*. Grand Rapids: W. B. Eerdmans, 1982. A well-illustrated guide to the history of church architecture.

Davies, J. G. *Temples, Churches and Mosques*. New York: Pilgrim Press, 1982. A guide to the history and appreciation of religious architecture.

Davies, J. G., ed. *The Westminster Dictionary of Worship*. Philadelphia: Westminster Press, 1979. A helpful dictionary of liturgical terms.

Lutheran Book of Worship—Ministers Edition. Minneapolis and Philadelphia: Augsburg Pub. House and Lutheran Church in America Board of Publication, 1978. The LBW altar book (also available in a smaller desk edition) which contains complete rubrics, calendar details, and propers.

Moffitt, Oleta Staley. *Arranging Flowers for the Church*. Rev. ed. Philadelphia: Fortress Press, 1977. A guide to flower arrangements for use in worship.

Nitschke, Beverley, and Stephen Swenson. *With This Bread and Cup.* Philadelphia: Parish Life Press, 1985. A commentary on the Holy Communion liturgy in the *Lutheran Book of Worship.*

Occasional Services. Minneapolis and Philadelphia: Augsburg Pub. House and Lutheran Church in America Board of Publication, 1982. A companion volume to the *Lutheran Book of Worship,* containing rites for installations, dedications, the ministry of healing, and other occasional services.

Olsen, Mary P. *For the Greater Glory: A Church Needlepoint Handbook.* New York: Seabury Press, 1980. A helpful guide for those who do church needlework.

Pfatteicher, Philip H. *Commentary on the Occasional Services.* Philadelphia: Fortress Press, 1983. A commentary on all of the rites in *Occasional Services.*

————. *Festivals and Commemorations.* Minneapolis: Augsburg Pub. House, 1980. A handbook to the calendar of festivals and commemorations in the *Lutheran Book of Worship.*

Pfatteicher, Philip H., and Carlos R. Messerli. *Manual on the Liturgy.* Minneapolis: Augsburg Pub. House, 1979. A practical manual on preparing for and leading all of the rites in the *Lutheran Book of Worship.*

Podhradsky, Gerhard. *New Dictionary of the Liturgy.* Staten Island, N.Y.: Alba House, 1966. A helpful dictionary of liturgical terms.

Post, W. Elwood. *Saints, Signs, and Symbols.* 2d ed. Wilton, Conn.: Morehouse-Barlow Co., 1974. Illustrated guide to Christian symbols.

Raynor, Louise, and Carolyn Kerr. *Church Needlepoint.* Wilton, Conn.: Morehouse-Barlow Co., 1974. Practical guide to needlepoint for church use.

Stauffer, S. Anita. *Lutherans at Worship.* Minneapolis and Philadelphia: Augsburg Pub. House and Lutheran Church in America Board of Publication, 1978. An introduction to the *Lutheran Book of Worship.*

Stulken, Marilyn Kay. *Hymnal Companion to the Lutheran Book of Worship.* Philadelphia: Fortress Press, 1981. Provides information about the text and music of every hymn in the *Lutheran Book of Worship.*

Van Loon, Ralph R. *Parish Worship Handbook.* Philadelphia: Parish Life Press, 1979. A guide for all who have responsibility for planning and leading parish worship: church council, worship committee, pastor, assisting ministers, musicians, acolytes, ushers, and altar guild.

————. *Space for Worship.* Rev. ed. Philadelphia: Lutheran Church in America Division for Parish Services, 1982. A brief but helpful guide to architecture and art for worship.

Weiser, Francis X. *Handbook of Christian Feasts and Customs.* New York: Harcourt, Brace & World, 1958. An interesting guide to the history and customs of the festivals and seasons of the church year.

Index